Strides of Integrity and Honor

The Life of *James W. McCulloh* and His Family

by Lynn Scott

Strides of Integrity and Honor
The Life of James W. Mcculloh and His Family

Copyright ©2016 by Lynn Scott

ISBN 978-0-692-83374-2

All rights reserved. This book or any portion thereof may not be reproduced or used in any manner whatsoever without the express written permission of the publisher except for the use of brief quotations in a book review.

Cover Photo: View of Baltimore, Maryland from Federal Hill, drawn and engraved by E. Whitefield, lithograph by F. Michlen, ca. 1847, Library of Congress

Book design by www.StoriesToTellBooks.com

"It is true that to attention must be added the strides of integrity & honor for a man without these stands very low in the rank of this life. I shall strive to adhere to them…"

—James W. McCulloh
23 December 1809

Contents

Chapter 1 "A Child of Sorrow" *1*

Chapter 2 Life as Child *9*

Chapter 3 Service in the War of 1812 *19*

Chapter 4 A Family of Ten *21*

Chapter 5 Heading in a Different Direction *31*

Chapter 6 A Tragic End *39*

Chapter 7 The Civil War and Beyond *43*

Chapter 8 Grandchildren, a Lasting Legacy *51*

Chapter 9 The British Connection *63*

Appendix McCulloh Family Lineage *65*

Notes *81*

Index *119*

Chapter 1

"A Child of Sorrow"

James W. McCulloh never knew his mother. She died February 19, 1789, when he was only two weeks old. His full name, James William Benoi Todd McCulloh, reflects the event with "Benoi" meaning child of sorrow. His father, John McCulloh, was devastated that his wife of eighteen years was no longer with him.[1]

Concerned about John and how he would care for the eight young children at home, his brother James, namesake for James W., wrote from Baltimore, "Remember your health and their [the children's] future happiness. Guard against that melancholy." James also took on the responsibility of finding help for John. He made arrangements for their niece Isabella Williamson to move from Baltimore to Philadelphia to be a temporary housekeeper.[2]

John had married Anna Todd in 1771. A little over a year later, he rented pew number 40 at the newly formed Third Presbyterian Church of

Old Pine Church – line drawing by Ronald E. Shaffer, based on period discriptions, Courtesy of Old Pine Conservancy

Rev. George Duffield, Courtesy of Old Pine Conservancy

Philadelphia. Located at the corner of 4th and Pine, the church was only one block from their home. He may have originally joined out of convenience, but he soon became involved with a group of members to call a new pastor, Rev. George Duffield. They had heard that this preacher from Carlisle in the Pennsylvania frontier was unconventional and a "New Light."[3]

Finding the door locked when he arrived to preach his first sermon on September 27, 1772, Rev. Duffield was not deterred. With the help of parishioners, he "entered the church through a rear window." His rousing sermons drew many, including John Adams, who "went often to hear him preach" when in town. Duffield's patriotism was well known and in 1777 he was chosen as co-chaplain of the Continental Congress. Because of Duffield and the fact that over 200 men from the congregation participated in the Revolution, the Third Presbyterian Church became known as "The Church of the Patriots." Today it is referred to as Old Pine Church.[4]

John took an oath of allegiance on June 26, 1777, and shortly thereafter, on August 27, was commissioned as captain of an artillery company in Jehu Eyre's regiment of the Pennsylvania militia. That September John's company of 32 artillery men was mustered into Fort Mifflin, a fortification on the marshy ground of Mud Island, just south of Philadelphia along the Delaware River. Here roughly 200 men were charged with holding back a fleet of British ships loaded with supplies bound for General Howe's army that had triumphantly marched into Philadelphia.[5]

The Fort Mifflin website describes what happened:

> On frozen, marshy ground within the walls of a stone and wood fort, the American Revolution produced a shining moment. Cold, ill and starving, the young garrison of (now) 400 men at Fort Mifflin refused to give up. The valiant efforts of the men at Fort Mifflin held the mighty British Navy at bay providing Washington and his troops time to arrive safely at Valley Forge where they shaped a strong and confident army. This battle escalated into the greatest bombardment of the American Revolution and one that many say changed the course of American History.
>
> For nearly six weeks in the fall of 1777, American troops in Fort Mifflin and Fort Mercer frustrated British naval attempts to re-supply their occupying forces in Philadelphia.... On November 15th, finally clear after days of rain and high tides, the British sailed the Vigilant and Fury, with nineteen cannon up the back channel to the west of Fort Mifflin. In the main channel of the Delaware three ships armed with 158 cannon anchored directly offshore of the fort, while to the east three additional ships armed with 51 cannon completed the naval assault.
>
> Against this show of force, Fort Mifflin could respond with only ten cannon. It was reported that during one hour, 1,000 cannon balls were fired at the fort ... Exhausted, cold and out of ammunition, Major Simeon Thayer evacuated Fort Mifflin's garrison to Fort Mercer with muffled oars after nightfall on November 15.[6]

McCulloh's unit was enlisted for six weeks, but many stayed longer. A "paper dated Nov. 18, 1777, contains an inventory of stores under the care of Capt. McCulloh," which means he would have been at the fort until their evacuation.[7] Most likely, John returned to Philadelphia after his time at Fort

Model of British ships attacking Fort Mifflin, taken at Fort Mifflin National Historic Landmark Museum

Mifflin—since militia often served in two or three month increments—returning home to care for business and family in between.

John's pension file states that he fought at the Battle of Brandywine, but that does not seem possible, since the Pennsylvania militia records record his company mustering in at Fort Mifflin on September 10th and the Battle of Brandywine started on September 11th. The confusion may come through his commanding officer, Col. Jehu Eyre, who took two companies with him to Brandywine and ordered his other two companies to fortifications on the Delaware.

McCulloh's men obviously went to fortify Fort Mifflin.[8] The same situation probably applies to the battles of Trenton and Princeton. Col. Eyre was at both, but even though John's pension credits him with being at the battles of Trenton and Princeton, no evidence to support that has been found.[9]

On April 27, 1779, John was once again called up, this time as Captain of 55 men under Col. Eyre. The British had left Philadelphia the previous year, and John and his men were sent to Billingsport. While there he wrote to Joseph Reed, president of the Continental Congress:

Billingsport, May 5, 1779

May it please your Excellency,
In consequence of your orders to the City Lieutenant, I arrived her the 2d instant and relieved the detachment of Col. Procter's Artilery at this post, and alongst with the command I recd your instructions to them, wherein I find it my duty to report to you what ever may be necessary to be done. I would therefore beg leave to communicate to you that our Ammunition is in a very dangerous deposit at present, which is an apartment adjoining the Barracks, and is therefore liable, by the smallest accident of fire, to be blown up, which might be fatal to the whole garrison; neither is it water tight. There is another part of your instructions which direct that the officer commanding here should treat the officers of all inward bound vessels, whether Americans or Allies, with kindness & respect, but when I made a small draught upon the Commissary, in order to enable me to fulfill that part of the order, he peremptorily refused it, though he acknowledged the necessity there was for it, but said he could not Issue it without an order from you or the Honble, the Board of War, either of which he would immediately obey, and of choice I would much rather apply to your Excellency; I beg therefore you would communicate your pleasure in a line, and if you are pleased to indulge me, as I humbly hope you will, as it is common to officers in my situation, be assured it shall be conducted with becoming frugality.

I am, Sir, with the most profound respect,
Your Excellency's most obedient
And very Humble Sarvent,
JOHN M'CULLOH
Capt Comd

P.S. There are a great number of my Compy Mechanicks, which would Immediately go to work upon a Magazine if there was one to be built, and my assistance shall not be wanting.[10]
J. M'C"

Ammunition magazine at Fort Mifflin National Historic Landmark

John McCulloh was promoted to Major of the Artillery Battalion, April 15, 1780, and he was called into service August 10, 1780, commanding the City of Philadelphia and District Militia. He commanded in 1782 and 1786, as well. For his service during the Revolution, John received four tracts of land in western Pennsylvania which were used as a source of timber for his business.[11]

To raise money for the war, the city of Philadelphia, through the Redemption of the Bills of Credit enacted March 25, 1780, "claimed all of Penn's unsold property in the city and sold it at public auction, the proceeds going to military supplies." Burial spaces at Third Presbyterian Church cemetery had reached near capacity, so in 1782 John and Anna bought two lots being sold by the city that were adjacent to the church. They immediately transferred the property to three men from the church to be used as a burying ground "subject to the annual delivery of one acorn."[12]

Listed among family papers are numerous documents by individuals appointing John McCulloh as their attorney or executor. His main occupation, however, involved a business with his four brothers importing mahogany, rum, silk, china, tea, and more. "John, Joseph and brother-in-law, Edward Pannell, were based in Philadelphia. William captained the family ship *Prosperity* ... James settled in Baltimore where he was a member" of Knox, Usher and McCulloh.[13] Even though most of these men would be gone before James W. McCulloh came of age, the men running the family business would influence his career.

Toward the end of the 1700s, American merchant ships were being attacked by the French. On March 9, 1796, the French captured one of John's ships, the brig *Anna*. The loss of 4,609 pounds of merchandise was a blow to the family business. After peace was made, the family submitted a claim to France in 1804, but it is doubtful they ever recovered the money.[14]

In the fall of 1798, John and his oldest son, Samuel, whom he called Samey, set out on a six-week journey to western Pennsylvania and Pittsburgh. Whether it was for business purposes or to check on his properties is not known, but John was impressed with the area and seriously considered moving there. A letter from son Andrew to his sister Isabella says father was "much pleased with the many beauties of the Western Country – there is now nothing wanting but Mama's consent to move – how she will decide I know not but am in hopes she will meet his wishes." Since the family stayed in Philadelphia, she obviously rejected the idea of moving to what she called "the wilderness." Had they made the move, life for James W. McCulloh might have turned out differently.[15]

Chapter 2
Life as Child

James W. McCulloh grew up in a bustling, affluent household. A year after the death of his mother, James' father remarried to a second woman named Anna, Anna Bringhurst, daughter of John and Elizabeth (Shute) Bringhurst. To an already abundant household would be added eight more children from this second marriage. She became a loving stepmother who

John McCulloh home in Philadelphia, "Spruce Street, 1st house East of 4th Street"

Inventory of the personal estate of John McCulloh, April 28, 1800, Courtesy of the Maryland Historical Society, Item ID MS 2110

guided and corresponded with all of the children into and throughout their adulthood, signing her letters, "affectionately Mother."[16]

The family lived in a three-story house, one room wide and three rooms deep, at 214 Spruce Street in Philadelphia, just east of 4th. Tax records indicate a stable, as well. From the inventory done at his father's death, an image of how the rooms were used emerges. The front parlor appeared to be an office of sorts with a mahogany desk and bookcase, two card tables, and six chairs. The back parlor was family living space with a mahogany dining table, a breakfast table, six side chairs, a Windsor chair, and a sofa. Behind the two parlors were a kitchen and a wash house. All rooms in the house had a carpet, a looking glass, and the appropriate brass andirons and tools for a fireplace. The entryway had a carpet, as well. There was silver plate, candlesticks, glassware and Queensware, all speaking to a gracious lifestyle.[17]

The front room on the second floor must have been a bedroom for John and Anna since it held only one bed with curtains. A mahogany chest of drawers, a mahogany bureau, an easy chair, and a warming pan completed the room. The back chamber was probably shared by the younger children in the family, since it had two mahogany beds and one poplar bed, a mahogany bureau, and six chairs. Behind the bedrooms was a store room with a chest "containing Sunday clothing," three trunks, and extra bedding.

The third floor had three rooms, each with a bed. There was also a mahogany bed chair, a chest of drawers, two dressing tables, and four chairs among them. These bedrooms may have been used by the older children, giving them space of their own.

A diary of family expenses kept by James' stepmother, Anna, sheds light on the family lifestyle. Every other day Anna walked four blocks to Market Street to purchase fresh groceries. This was common, since farmers from the outlying farms brought produce into the city, eliminating the need for residents to grow their own vegetables or raise livestock. Money paid to merchants attests to the variety of food at their table. They ate beef, pork, turkey, partridges, mutton, and fish, used white flour, buckwheat, cornmeal, and rye flour, and had such niceties as coffee, French brandy, oysters, and chocolate. In addition to food, Anna purchased gloves and a wig for her daughter Mary, cotton stripe fabric for pantaloons, and a "puncheon of sewing silk."[18]

Map of Phildelphia, 1796 showing the McCulloh house (Letter H) and Third Presbyterian Church (Letter C) - Taken from a Plan of the city of Philadelphia and its environs showing the improved parts by John Hills and John Cooke, Library of Congress

Shoes were in constant need, and it appears they owned more than 1 pair each. One bill for the year 1794 showed 8 pairs of shoes being rebound and given new heels, along with the purchase of 19 new pairs of shoes. This for a household of 13 people.[19]

Fortunately, the family survived the almost yearly yellow fever outbreaks—which showed up each fall—without loss of life. They would "flee to the Bringhursts' home in Germantown." In the particularly bad year of 1802, Mary wrote her brother Andrew that, "Uncle Bringhurst ... says he was obliged to come [out of Philadelphia] because all his acquaintances had left him and there was no business a doing, for our City never was so soon deserted. Had it not been so it is supposed it would have been very fatal this season but several families have been so imprudent as to return and have been taken ill."[20]

James was only 11 when his father suffered a stroke paralyzing his left side

Tablet and pedestal gravestone of John and Anna McCulloh, Old Pine Church Cemetery

leading to his death. His brother Dr. Samuel McCulloh wrote, "Major John McCulloh ... who was killed by 11 stubborn fools of a jury who would not give a just verdict and kept the Major shut up forty-eight hours in a long room which brought on apoplexy of which he died in 1800."[21] John was buried in the graveyard property he had purchased for Old Pine Church. James would later recall "the many good instructions of a departed parent, whose name shall ever be dear to me." It is "an honor to me to hear his name who was [an] affectionate and worthy Father."[22]

In his will John left his wife "all his household goods," the remaining indenture of three servants, a horse, cow, silver they had purchased, and "150 pounds current money." To his oldest son, Samuel, he gave his silver tankart; his "personal trinkets" were to be divided among his other three sons. The silver belonging to his first wife he left to her daughters, Anne, Mary, and Margaret. He left $20 as her share to his daughter Elizabeth from his first marriage. The remainder of his estate was to be sold and invested in either Bank Stock of Pennsylvania or public stock of the United States, producing income that would be divided into thirds. One third to his wife, the remaining two-thirds divided between his named children: Samuel, Andrew, John, James, George, Robert, Isaac, Anne, Mary, Margaret, Sarah, and Isabella. Why Elizabeth is not included in this list is not known.[23]

John McCulloh's estate was valued at $36,415, which in today's money would be worth somewhere around $709,000, using the percentage increase in the Consumer Price Index. $5,263 was in cash at the Bank of Pennsylvania, and he had $3,669 tied up in an "adventure of [the] Ship Canton," which is assumed to mean its cargo. Approximately a quarter of his wealth was in lumber and mahogany boards, the remainder, besides his house and contents, being in money due from customers. The properties owned in western Pennsylvania were not mentioned.[24]

As happens today, settling an estate does not always go easy. John's wife, Anna, and his two oldest sons, Samuel and Andrew, were the executors. Samuel wrote to Andrew on May 16th, 1800:

Dear Brother,
… Not an individual has come forward since you left us to purchase a single article offered for sale, this circumstance induces me to think that our expectations concerning them were rather sanguine. I have offered the mahogany to Mr. Willings & Frances but do not find them disposed either to purchase or to allow my permission to send any of it out in their ship to Bengal.[25]

A follow up letter a week later said:

Dear Brother,
… I was very apprehensive and I should be obliged to make considerable sacrifices of it to the grumbling tribe of petty dealers in the article, a numerous posse of whom attended [the sale] … their expectations were perhaps never more completely disappointed than on this occasion … Mr. Frances … (who was I believe … acquainted with the quality of wood) came forward just before the sale was to have commenced and proposed taking the whole of the mahogany.… .

… Last week I sold the coaches for $200 cash, the sleigh to Mr. Bently for $16. The horses are still on hand and will part with them if enough to say I haven't given them away… being comparably tired of waiting for a reasonable offer.[26]

John's death left the family with reduced finances, although hardly poor. The loss of the brig *Anna*, combined with unrecoverable assets from John's estate, meant limited investments producing funds to live on. James W.'s oldest brother, Samuel, helped support Anna and the remaining children at home for the rest of their lives. He faithfully sent $200 a month.[27]

James probably expected to follow in his father's footsteps as a merchant. At the age of 12, he took his future into his own hands, and on the one year anniversary of his father's death, he wrote to his brother in Baltimore:

April 13, 1801

Dear Brother,
Brother Samuel in a letter from you some time ago, in which you mentioned there was a vacancy in one of Mr. Pierce's dry goods stores, that you thought it would be a more eligible situation for me than where I now am. That Mr. Pierce was willing for me to fill that vacancy – Sammy mentioned it to Mr. Knox – he said he had no objections to it. I have asked Mr. Knox when it would suit him to let me go down – having all my things ready – he says he would like me to stay until the schooner Roun returned from Cape Francis … it may be two or three weeks most likely before I could leave him, but he says if it is necessary for me to go down this week he has no objections to it – therefore I would thank you to let me know by return post when it is necessary for me to be there – I shall be guided by your reply –

Remain yours affectionately, J. W. McCulloh[28]

By August 1801 James was living in Baltimore. Letters sent back and forth between Philadelphia and Baltimore give an account of the family's activities. Usually carried by family or friends traveling between the two cities, only on rare occasion would letters be mailed by post. His stepmother wrote, "James … being so young, I have not asked him what business he means to study; Mr. Weston speaks highly of his abilities and attention to his studies."[29]

Philaa. 13th April 1801

Dear Brother

Brother Samuel recd. a letter from you some time ago, in which you mentioned there was a vacancy in one of Mr. Pine's dry good stores, that you thought it would be a more eligible situation for me than where I now am, that Mr. Pine was willing for me to fill that vacancy — Sammy mentioned it to Mr. Knox — He said he had no objections to it — I have asked Mr. Knox when it would suit him to let me go down — having all my things ready — he says he would like me to stay untill the schooner Brown returns from Cape Francois, which he thinks will be in a week or ten days and it may be two or three weeks most likely before I could leave him, but he says if it is necessary for me to go down this week he has no objections to it — therefore I would thank you to let me know by return of Post — when it is

Original letter of James W. McCulloh, age 12, April 13, 1801, Courtesy of the Maryland Historical Society, Item ID MS 2110

Original letter of James W. McCulloh, age 12, April 13, 1801, Courtesy of the Maryland Historical Society, Item ID MS 2110

James initially lived with two of his single brothers, Andrew and John. Sister Mary wrote, "I wish you would send up all your old shirts that want mending by John. Make James gather up all of his clothes that want mending and I wish you to desire John to do the same and bring them along." When the mending no longer sufficed, James' sisters provided new clothes. Margaret wrote, "Be so good as to tell James if the shirt we have sent him fits, the others shall be made like it, this he must inform us of soon if he is in need of them."[30]

Like many teenagers, James decided to try things on his own. While his intentions were admirable, he was not always prudent. An undated letter from Andrew to Anna says that James had moved out from under his brother's wings to another location, was buying his own clothes, and attending a French school. Andrew mentions that he could have procured "him a situation in some French family where he would have a much better opportunity of acquiring the language." James must have run up other debts because Andrew says, I "immediately paid off every cent he owed, even a balance against him at Akins Books." This does not seem to have upset Andrew, because he continues, "I do not mean to take any particular merit to myself for I consider I have only acted as one Brother would towards another and have mentioned it to you to share the difference. There is something to be met with in the disposition of brothers. James I believe possesses an honest a principal as John did."[31]

Customary of the time, merchants received an education in a counting house, and James eventually studied at the counting house of George Williams. It is not clear if this was a type of apprenticeship, but in 1810 Anna writes, "Give my love to James. Tell him I should be pleased to see him as he is a freeman."[32]

At the end of his schooling in 1809, he told his brother, "May I ever be guided by [my father's] instructions, follow the paths which he has followed and laid open to us." He also mentions "the profession and situation which I have made choice of for my future." He talks of serving Mr. Knox, a former partner of his uncle, and the business knowledge Mr. Knox will impart to him, but unfortunately doesn't say specifically what that is.[33]

Chapter 3

Service in the War of 1812

George Sears, a customer of one of James' employers, had a lovely daughter named Abigail who caught James' attention. Family described her as "a highly refined, sweet and articulate woman."[34] James married Abigail Sears at the First Methodist Episcopal Church in Baltimore, Maryland, on May 19, 1814.

Less than two months later James joined the Baltimore United Volunteers, part of the 5th Regiment of the Maryland Militia in the War of 1812. A corporal in Captain Warfield's Company, he was wounded at the Battle of Bladensburg on August 24, 1814, when American troops failed in trying to stop the British from reaching the capital of Washington, D.C. "This engagement, often derisively referred to as the 'Bladensburg Races,' left the nation's capital defenseless."[35]

A firsthand account of the Battle of Bladensburg comes from the autobiography of John Pendleton Kennedy:

It was a day of glorious anticipation, that Sunday morning; when with all the glitter of a dress parade, we set forth on our march. As we moved through the streets, the pavements were crowded with anxious spectators; the windows were filled with women; friends were rushing to the ranks to bid us good-bye – many exhorting us to be of good cheer … What a scene it was … This was a real army marching to a real war. My feet were swollen and sore from my day's march in boots, such as none but a green soldier would ever have put on; so for my comfort, I had taken them off and substituted my neat pair of pumps from the pocket of my knapsack … [After a short night] we were ordered forthwith to break up our camp and march towards Washington. Here was new excitement – everything was gathered up in a few moments. All our baggage was tossed into our regimental wagon – knapsacks, provisions, blankets, everything but our arms. Among them went my boots. At length when we had reached a hill some three miles on our route, we were marched into a stubble field and told we might rest until daylight.

Our orders then were to march back to Bladensburg. Soon we had the famous 'trial of souls' – the battle of Bladensburg. The drafted militia ran away at the first fire, and the 5th regiment was driven off the field with the bayonet. We made a fine scamper of it. I lost my musket in the melee while bearing off a comrade, James W. McCulloch, afterwards the cashier of the Branch Bank of the United States in Baltimore, whose leg was broken by a bullet. The day was very hot and the weight of my wounded companion great, and not being able to carry both, I gave my musket to a friend who accompanied me and he, afterwards being wounded himself, dropped his own weapon as well as mine.[36]

According to his daughter-in-law Anna (Austen) McCulloch, this wound caused James to walk on crutches for seven years.[37]

Chapter 4
A Family of Ten

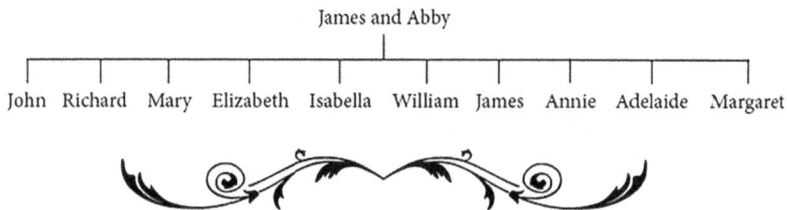

James' and Abby's first child, John Sears McCulloch, was born in 1816. With son Richard Sears, born in 1818, and daughter Mary Louisa on the way, James bought a 511-acre farm and built a large stone farmhouse, which is now part of the Community College of Baltimore in Catonsville. The land, cleared by the former owners, had an apple orchard of 500 trees which produced enough fruit for eating and cider to pay the interest on the mortgage each year. There was a stable, stone dairy, slave quarters, and four tobacco barns. Many of the fields were divided by stone walls. The 1820 census shows James had six slaves, six free colored persons, and two white men to work his farm. Presumably, daughters Elizabeth Ann and Isabella Williamson were born on the farm, since they were born in 1822 and 1825, respectively. After the foreclosure on this property, James moved his family to Baltimore, living in a house between Green and Paca streets.[38]

The summer Isabella was two years old she suffered an accident that crippled her right hand for life. Her Irish nurse was not paying attention when Isabella grabbed a stick supporting a large sash window, which fell and crushed her hand. "Her uncle Dr. S[amuel] McCulloh carefully watched her

Stone farmhouse built by James W. McCulloh, now part of the Community College of Baltimore, Catonsville, Maryland

to prevent any deformity of the hand." A leather form was made to bind up her hand, preserving the shape.[39]

A delicate child, Isabella began to develop a crooked spine at about age six or seven, causing a "nervous disturbance." The curvature of the spine may have been inherited since her Uncle Isaac suffered from the same disorder at about the same age. This problem made it necessary for Isabella's schooling to be done at home. James hired "the very best teachers he could find in Baltimore" for sisters Mary and Isabella. They were taught French, dancing, music, and mathematics, among other subjects. Speaking of their lives as children, Mary said, "Belle and I shared everything, had one room, were dressed alike, and went everywhere together."[40]

As busy as his career kept him, James was not all work. His family adored him, and his "chief relaxation in his busy life" was spending time with the family. There was an "element of merry playfulness, which found its outlet in familiar, joyous intercourse with his children." Five more children would be added to the family over the next nine years: twins William James and James William in 1827, Annie Lucretia in 1829, Adelaide Sears in 1831, and Margaret in 1834."[41]

Shows Paca and Green St. in the upper left section. Taken from the Plan of the city of Baltimore, 1836, by Fielding Lucas, Jr., Library of Congress

As the boys reached the appropriate age, James sent them off to college. The two oldest, John and Richard, "attended the classical department of the University of Maryland" where their Aunt Margaret commented, "Chemistry seems to be Richard's favorite [subject] at present." That interest would last a lifetime and establish Richard's career. After leaving the University of

Maryland, they went to the College of New Jersey (later to become Princeton University). John graduated in 1835, 11th in his class, and Richard, who showed exceptional intelligence at an early age, graduated a year later at age 18, "ranking fourth in a class of sixty-six." "From family letters [Richard] emerges as a young man of great self-confidence and wit. Adventurous by nature, he also possessed the wonderful knack of making people feel good about themselves."[42] Following his schooling, Richard went to Philadelphia to study chemistry with James Curtis Booth.[43]

Younger brother William graduated in 1843 from Jefferson College in Canonsburg, Pennsylvania. His attendance there is not surprising since his father was a trustee, and his brother Richard by that time was on the faculty.[44]

Mary was the first child to marry. Her husband, Henry Christian Mayer, graduated from Harvard in 1838 and was an attorney in Baltimore when they married in 1842. They lived in a home on Madison St. with eight acres "under cultivation as a Market Garden." A newspaper description says, "The dwelling has two kitchens and a servant's room in the basement, two large parlors on the first floor and four chambers on the second floor and … two large garret rooms for servants."[45]

A little over a year after their marriage, Mary and Henry moved to Mayville, New York. Shortly thereafter, they blessed James and Abby with their first grandchild, Susan Theresa Mayer. Henry Mayer, Jr. came in 1844, yet heartbreak was soon to follow. Their third child died an infant.

Then, at the early age of 25, Henry's health began to fail. He set out for New York City, seeking medical advice, but never made it. Henry died in his sleep of an enlarged heart at a hotel in Rochester, New York, while en route. Mary was three months pregnant with their fourth child at the time. After burying her husband, she and her two toddlers moved in with her parents, where her fourth child was born. Tragedy would strike again when Mary's oldest daughter, Susan Theresa, died in 1857 at the age of 13 from scarlet fever.[46]

To start his new position as Comptroller, James moved his family from Baltimore to Washington, D.C. One of James' sons wrote, "When first the family resided at Washington, it was in the gay circle of fashion, at presidential levees, ministerial receptions, etc." His daughter Margaret had this to say: "The following winter, by father's request, Belle [Isabella] went with him a good

Inauguration ball, Treasury Department, Washington, D.C., from a sketch by James E. Taylor, 1869, Library of Congress

deal into society, and being the oldest daughter at home, she relieved mother, whose health was delicate, of the social claims her position imposed."[47]

This was a busy time for the family. Abby's mother, Lucretia (Fry) Sears, lived with them until her death in 1845, helping with the younger children and busy social schedule. To her grandmother, Isabella "was ever the pet lamb of all the flock." Mrs. Sears enjoyed being involved in Isabella's life, "was happy in assisting her in her dressing and preparations for society and in listening to her spirited recitals of what she saw there." Before her grandmother died, she suffered "an illness of many weeks," for which Isabella was her "constant and devoted nurse." "It was during those days when she for the first time watched face to face with death, that Isabella determined to be a Christian." "She immediately became an earnest worker in the Sunday school ... [and] gathered a class of twenty colored women, who listened to her story of Jesus with grateful earnestness."[48]

The family attended Trinity Church, where the rector, Dr. Butler, "was much loved by the family." There, daughter Adelaide met her future husband, John P. Hubbard, who was at the time superintendent of the Sunday school. They married while he was a student at the Episcopal Theological Seminary in Alexandria, Virginia. Afterward, they made plans to go to China, and Isabella was anxious to go with them. Her delicate health made her father request that Isabella stay home, but the trip to China never materialized.[49]

Being married to an Episcopal minister, Adelaide's family moved 4 times, taking the pastorate at various churches. After her husband, John Hubbard, graduated from seminary, they went to Northampton, Massachusetts, where 3 children were born, including little Margaret, who died at the age 3. They lost two other children—John's namesake before he reached age 7 and William before he was age 2. A second son named John P. disappeared from the records after age 19, so he may have died as well.

John's next assignment was to Westerly, Rhode Island, for approximately ten years, where three more children were born. His last pastorate was in Potomac, West Virginia.[50]

Through John Hubbard, his sister-in-law Isabella "became acquainted with families of professors" at the Theological Seminary, spending much time and companionship discussing spiritual growth. In a letter written between 1850 and 1852, she wrote, "To live for the glory of our God and Savior, how it ennobles life and robs its sorrows."[51]

Isabella married late in life. After returning from a trip to Switzerland, she spent a lot of time at her sister Adelaide's home. "There she renewed her acquaintance with [Rev. John Singleton Copley] Greene, whom she had met years before at her father's house in Washington … They became engaged and were married in the Church of the Ascension in New York City" by Adelaide's husband, Rev. Hubbard. Isabella's husband, like Adelaide's, was an Episcopal minister. This was his third marriage, and Isabella moved to his home in Brookline, Massachusetts, where she helped raise his two teenage children still at home. Her "education and culture, her experience of refined social life, and her labors in the church and among the poor" prepared her for new duties as a minister's wife. "The high social position of her husband … brought her into relations with many persons … Not infrequently she spent the morning in distributing the necessities of life in the cottages of the poor and the evening with friends whose surroundings would make one forget that poverty had an existence."[52]

Not surprisingly, James' children inherited or learned various traits from him: a strong work ethic, a keen business sense, his drive, sharp intelligence, perseverance, religious interest, and the desire to give back to the community.

Like his father, John Sears McCulloch became a prominent lawyer in Baltimore, having studied under John V. L. McMahon. Unlike other members of the family, he used the "ch" spelling of the McCulloch name. In 1844 John married Anna Austen, daughter of George and Caroline (Millemon) Austen, at the Associate Reformed Church in Baltimore. Soon after their marriage the young couple went to live with his parents in Washington, D.C. Five years later, "John and Anna moved from Washington to New York City, where his business became that of a commercial and maritime lawyer." To accommodate his growing family, John purchased a home in Southfield on Staten Island.[53]

New York City, the center of commerce, gradually drew other members of the family. Son James William McCulloh started his career there, working as a clerk for Howland and Aspinwall, an East India firm. He married Isabella Steel Walker on December 19, 1850, and early in their marriage they lived at 32 W. 29th Street. With the completion of the Hudson River Railroad in 1849, it became possible for men of means to live outside the city and commute to work. With two young children, James must have found this idea tempting, because he moved his family north of the city to Riverdale.[54]

William Lewis Morris, a wealthy New York City attorney, had built a Greek Revival home in 1836 in Riverdale, overlooking the Hudson River. Now referred to as "Wave Hill," the Morrises left in 1852 after the death of his wife. The next owner did not buy the house until 1866. There are no records to substantiate that James rented this house in 1855 and 1856, but city directories show him living in Riverdale during those years, and a McCulloh family tradition saying his son Charles was born on the "Morris Farm" in 1856 could be referring to this property.[55]

Using his keen business sense, probably inherited from his grandfather, James William (the son) formed a partnership with Buckingham & Sons of Putnam, Ohio, creating the firm of Buckingham & McCulloh in New York City, merchants of wholesale produce goods. Unfortunately, the partnership only lasted two years, ending in a nasty lawsuit after the death of Philo Buckingham. "The Buckinghams insisted James was stealing from them; James believed they were holding out on him. Fearing the Buckinghams were in debt, James insisted upon holding onto the books." He claimed they still owed him $15,000 in commissions. "Testimony by the accountant and clerks in James' office seemed to corroborate his version [of] events."[56]

Whether he received the commissions he demanded is not known, but James William (the son) joined the Produce Exchange and continued on his own to become a successful broker of produce. He continued in this capacity for 20 years until accepting a position as receiver for the New Jersey Midland Railroad in 1876.[57]

Possibly through his father's connections in Washington, D.C., in December of 1845 Richard met and married Mary Stewart Vowell, daughter of Dr. John D. Vowell, who lived in Alexandria. Richard's only child, a daughter, who went by her middle name of Grace, was born two years later. On April 1, 1846, President James K. Polk appointed Richard as the "Melter and Refiner of the Mint of the United States at Philadelphia," an appointment he held until 1849.[58] While there he wrote several reports, among them the "Report of the Secretary of the Treasury of scientific investigations in relation to sugar and hydrometers."[59]

Though not involved in commerce, Richard Sears McCulloh would eventually join other family members in New York City. His switch to the academic world happened in 1849 when he accepted the position of Professor of Natural Philosophy, [science], at his old alma mater, the College of New Jersey. From there he moved to Columbia College in New York City as Professor of Mechanics and Physics. With numerous children in the New York City area, their father, James, moved to the City as well when he retired as Comptroller, taking up private law practice again.[60]

Although little is known of Annie, we do know that Annie Lucretia McCulloh married William Isaac Brown, a New York City merchant, in 1853. They lived outside the city in Orange, New Jersey, and he was apparently successful, since their home in 1860 was staffed with four servants.[61]

William James McCulloh moved farther afield. He shows up in the 1850 census, living in Ascension Parish, Louisiana, as a U.S. surveyor living with 5 other surveyors, all single men. He was appointed to the position of Surveyor General of the U.S. to the district of Louisiana by President Pierce in 1854. While living in Ascension, he met and married Adeline E. Bercegeay, daughter of Frenchman Alphonse Bercegeay. Three children came in quick succession,

2 apparently dying young. Two years after his marriage, a newspaper ad for a $500 reward was placed in 1858 when William's stable and carriage house was burnt. He lost the entire contents of both. The 1860 slave census showed he owned 3 slaves: 2 females, ages 32 and 48, and a male, age 42.[62]

James W. and his son William were not the only McCullohs to own slaves. James' brother Dr. Samuel McCulloh had a large plantation near Baltimore called Rockland. The 1830 census shows he had 9 slaves and 2 free colored men. One of those men was John Matthews. Matthews bound himself to Samuel for 12 years in exchange for Samuel buying Matthews' wife and 4 children at a cost of $1,000. In his will Samuel mentioned his slaves by name and age, specifying at what age they were to be freed. They included Fanny Matthews, age 42, with children Sarah, Martha, Mary, George, William, and Fanny; Mary Ann, with children Harriett and Emery; and James and Maria Smith with children Jane, Jim, David, Suck, and Dick.[63] Little did he know that slavery would end before the terms of his will expired.

Chapter 5
Heading in a Different Direction

After the War of 1812, the United States turned toward manufacturing, and a feeling of goodwill took place as the economy accelerated. On April 10, 1816, Congress chartered the Second Bank of the United States to help create a more stable financial situation. The Second Bank opened in Philadelphia in January of 1817, with branches in 18 other cities, including Baltimore, opening a few months later. Although he had expected to follow

United States Bank, Philadelphia, drawn by C. Burton, N.Y., engraved & printed by Fenner, Sears & Co., London, Library of Congress

his father into the merchant trade, James W. McCulloh's career headed in a different direction when he was appointed cashier of the Baltimore branch. In 1817 merchants were often called into the field of banking because they understood business and had local connections. Cashiers controlled the administration of the bank. An impressive position for a man who was just 27 years old. While preforming his duties at the bank, James studied law and was admitted to the bar in 1820.[64]

In this era of prosperity, land speculators and individuals borrowed large amounts of money. James, like many others, was speculating in stock. With ready cash in short supply, stock was put up as security for other stock purchases. In the McCulloh papers at the Maryland Historical Society are a series of 60-day promissory notes for amounts ranging from $1,000 to $3,000. Made out to James W. McCulloh, some had a 50-cent seal with an eagle in the center so presumably, they were for the bank and not him personally. In addition to these were promissory notes for which James himself borrowed money. Dated throughout 1818, 12 vouchers promised to pay sums of $250 and $1,000 in 60 days. A few were made out to Joseph Townsend, Treasurer of the Baltimore Equity Society.[65]

James and two of his friends, George Williams and James Buchanan, "borrowed $1.9 million from the Philadelphia branch [of the United States Bank], secured by 18,000 shares of bank stock at $100 par." During 1817 and 1818, he made regular trips from Baltimore to Philadelphia, most likely for banking business. Everything went smoothly until the financial Panic of 1819 when the United States Bank called in banknotes and started demanding cash payments.[66]

"Maryland had more banks than any other state in the union. Faced with demands for [currency] from out-of-state banks and the Second Bank, the Maryland banks and the people who used them became quite troubled. On February 11, 1818, Maryland passed a tax on bank notes not issued by banks chartered by the state." The tax could be avoided by paying an annual fee of $15,000, which as cashier of the only non-state bank, James refused to do. He then issued bank "notes to George Williams without paying the tax," and was fined $100. Thus began the major lawsuit of *McCulloch v. Maryland*, which resulted in a landmark decision by the United States Supreme Court.[67]

Chapter 5: Heading in a Different Direction

The State of Maryland took James to court, saying the Second Bank of the United States was required to pay the tax. He was convicted and fined $2,500. He appealed the case to the Maryland Court of Appeals, but "the Maryland Court of Appeals upheld the Maryland state tax law." James refused to give in. He again appealed, this time to the United States Supreme Court, with Daniel Webster, Attorney General, William Wirt and William Pinkney as lawyers for the bank. The case was argued for nine days, starting February 22, 1819. Chief Justice John Marshall delivered the decision of the court, which reversed the Maryland judgement. Not surprisingly, James was removed from his position at the bank in May of 1819. "At the time, McCulloh's accounts were about $150,000 in arrears."[68]

The new president of the Second Bank got James McCulloh, James Buchanan, and George Williams to agree to "furnish $900,000 security - $300,000 each" for the money borrowed against bank stock. "McCulloh lived up to his part of the bargain by getting 16 merchants to guarantee his notes, $12,500 each, and by offering his home for security." This eventually led to foreclosure on his farm when he defaulted on the mortgage. The property was auctioned in 1825, selling for $20,961, far below the $35,000 he paid for it.[69]

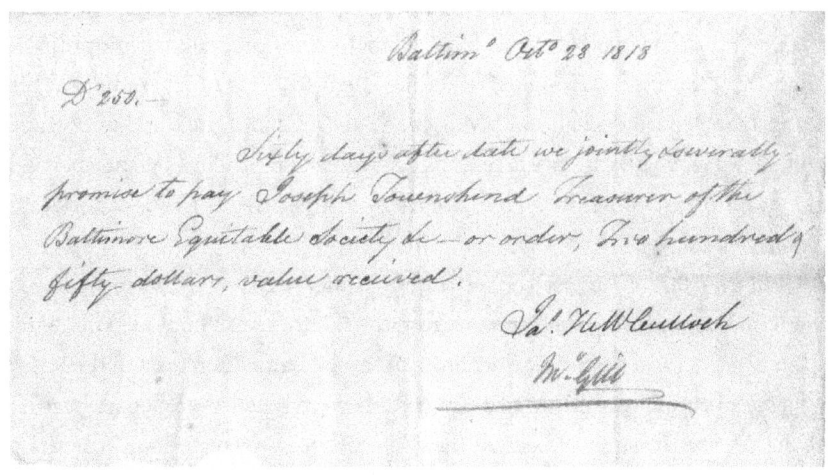

$250 Promisary note for James W. McCulloh, October 28, 1818, Courtesy of the Maryland Historical Society, Item ID MS 1356

With *McCulloch vs. Maryland* behind him, James faced another lawsuit. The *Alexandria Gazette* reported on April 12, 1823, that "the judges of the county court for Harford County, sitting at Bel Air have been engaged for the last three weeks in the trial of an indictment against James A. Buchanan, James W. McCulloh and Geo. Williams, charging them with a conspiracy to defraud the Bank of the U. States." The court acquitted all parties involved, saying they were doing nothing illegal, just speculating like the rest of the community.[70]

While facing these lawsuits, James suffered personal heartache as well. Daughter Elizabeth Ann was born May 11, 1822, dying two years later.[71]

Despite all his legal problems, James must have been well liked, because he was elected to the Maryland House of Delegates in 1825. Family had mixed feeling about this. Sister Margaret wrote to her brother Samuel, "[James] goes to Annapolis. He has my best wishes and sincere prayers for his success in which I am sure you join me, although you did not like his election any more than I did at first."[72]

The following year James became Speaker of the House and, during the 1827 legislative session, "pushed through" a bill incorporating the Baltimore and Ohio Railroad. One of the oldest railroads and the first common carrier in the country, the B&O provided a means of getting goods rapidly from the Ohio River Valley to the port of Baltimore. Competition from the Chesapeake and Ohio Canal fostered fights over land, labor, and fares. To settle conflicts between the feuding B&O and C&O Canal, James proposed a compromise that was "clear and reasonable," enabling them to reach an agreement. This important negotiation allowed Maryland's railroad and the canal to both be completed, giving Baltimore access to coal, wood, and produce in lands beyond the mountains, which in turn made them competitive with New York and Pennsylvania.[73]

On the 10th of August 1835, Baltimore suffered city-wide rioting. Crowds were upset over losing their money from the failure of the Bank of Maryland. They attacked and destroyed the homes of several bank directors and the home of Jesse Hunt, mayor of the city. Five people were killed. At a Senate hearing to discover what happened, James Blair gave his personal testimony, "…nothing would appease the infuriated mob, and restore peace and tranquility, except the immediate surrender (by the Trustees of the Bank of Maryland) of the books in their possession ..." The mayor called a meeting of highly respected citizens in the Council Chambers to figure out a way to quell the riots. Blair continued, "...great difference of opinion existed, and the resort to arms and peaceful measures were eloquently and forcibly discussed; but no decisive measure was adopted ... until a gentleman, James W. McCulloh, Esq. rose in his place, and by powerful reasoning on the policy of peaceful measures and an assurance that the books of the Bank of Maryland were not in the possession of the trustees, but on their way to Bell-air to be surrendered to the court, which would meet on the Monday following ... This, as regarded myself, and I believe many others, silenced the appeal to arms."[74]

James was good at mediation and, as lawyer for the family, became the middleman in a longstanding legal battle over his father's western lands. His older brother Samuel was the remaining executor to John McCulloh's estate and, after traveling to Western Pennsylvania, made detailed accounts of their father's acreage. Samuel listed 21 properties in 4 counties, totaling 5,218 acres of land. Trying to be a good steward, Samuel wanted to get the highest price possible on the sale of these lands, but "placed such high prices on them that they could not be sold." Between 1833 and 1837 Samuel received numerous bids for various properties, but his standard reply was, you offer "less than I am willing to take."[75]

As always in families, there were differences of opinions on how to handle things. James' siblings, particularly his unmarried sisters, became frustrated with the delay in settling the estate. In 1834 Sarah wrote to James, asking his professional opinion as to "the proper course to be pursued to bring about a settlement with our Brother Saml of the affairs of our deceased father's estate." William took matters into his own hands in 1836 by suing Samuel for money from the estate. He wrote to James saying, "You mention [Samuel] says in a few years he will be able to dispose of the lands to advantage – a little money will probably be of more service now than a larger sum a few years hence."[76]

By 1838 the sisters had hired a man named Robert Hord of Port Royal, Virginia, who was in the business of collecting "land bounty, pay or commutation and interest that may be due" on Revolutionary War services. They asked James to sign their petition against the State of Pennsylvania, but he must have declined, since his name does not appear on the paper.[77]

All of this caused strained feelings, and even though the estate lands were still not settled, James wrote a letter to Samuel in 1841 encouraging him to make amends. "If your health permits go to Anna in the morning ... The occasion presents the opportunity to forgive and I pray your pardon whilst I affectionately advise you in the goodness of your heart to forgive everyone." When Samuel died in 1848, the selling of the McCulloh lands in western Pennsylvania was taken over by James' son John.[78]

In addition to offering his services as a personal attorney, James was very involved in the community. Between 1828 and 1839 he was vice-president of the Whig party in Baltimore, secretary of the Franklin Turnpike Road, on the board of the Maryland State Penitentiary, and president of the Canton Company of Baltimore. He was also a trustee of the Promotion of Science and Literature and the University of Maryland and on the board of the Cross Cut Canal.[79]

Described in a newspaper account, a strange thing happened to James on September 20, 1839:

> We regret to lean that Mr. James W. McCulloh met with a serious accident yesterday morning, between the hours of three and four o'clock. Whilst asleep, a large portion of the ceiling, immediately over the bed, gave way, and one of the pieces of plastering struck him on the temple, severing the artery in that region. A surgeon was fortunately soon obtained and the artery tied. He was otherwise severely injured on the head, but his numerous friends will be glad to learn that he is already in a fair way to recover.[80]

The culmination of James' career came when President John Tyler appointed him to the office of First Comptroller of the United States Treasury in March of 1842. This important position required him to supervise all public accounts, including the recovery of money due the United States from lands, contracts, patents, and bonds, etc. and examine accounts settled by the 1st and 5th auditors and the Commissioner of the General Land Office. It involved an annual statement before Congress of accounts of the Treasury of War and Navy "that remained more than three years unsettled." His sister Isabella's

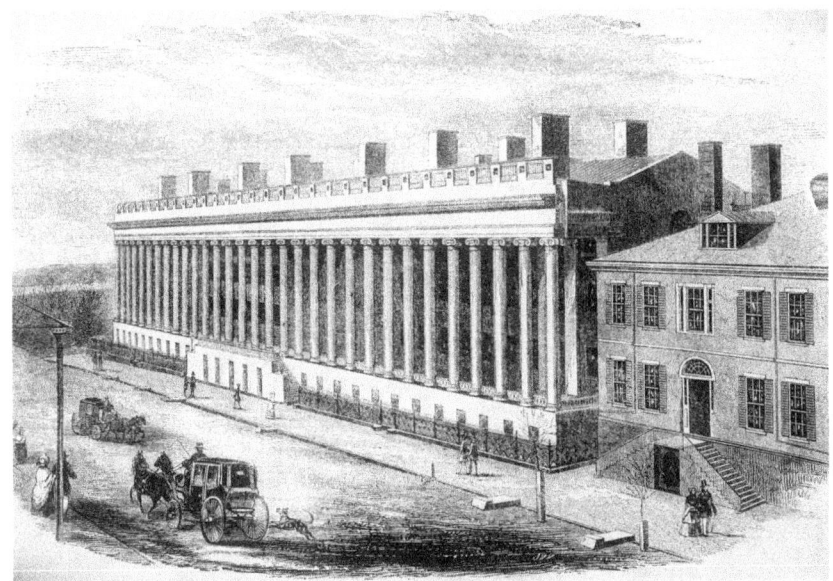

U.S. Treasury building, Washington, D.C., 1853, Library of Congress

husband, James S. Green, served at the same time, having been nominated by President Tyler as Secretary of the Treasury. James W. McCulloh filled his position as Comptroller during the administrations of both Tyler and James K. Polk. He resigned after President Zachary Taylor was elected.

In 1853 James and Abby moved from Washington, D.C. to New York City, probably to be closer to their children living there.[81]

Chapter 6

A Tragic End

By 1855 "James' sons were deeply concerned with his slowness" and started to take "an increased roll in management of his affairs." He and Abby moved in with their son Richard in New York City. From family letters it seems like James may have been suffering from Alzheimer's. If that was the case, James may have needed more attention than Richard's full schedule allowed, so James and Abby went to live with their daughter Annie and her husband, William Brown, in Orange, New Jersey. Sister Margaret also moved in with Annie to help care for their parents. Annie appears to have had the heart for taking care of others. Her aging and infirm parents lived with her until their deaths, and in 1870 she went to Massachusetts to help her brother-in-law, J.S. Copley Greene, care for his family after the death of her sister Isabella.[82]

James' son John talks about a visit to see his father in 1859. "Last night I was at Orange … My visits there are painful … the childlike spirit … breaks all my calmness down … I am walking in advance of the funeral of a mind …."[83]

Margaret had devoted so much time helping with the care of her father "that Abby sent her to Europe to recover her health and spirits." She traveled with her sister Isabella and husband on their trip to Switzerland in 1860. Isabella's husband, Rev. J.S. Copley Greene, was not well, and a trip to Europe had been prescribed to help him regain his strength. Hard as it was to leave her six-week-old daughter, Isabella decided the trip must be made but would be too hard on an infant. With Margaret going with them, Isabella called on older sister Mary to care for her newborn. Mary agreed and of course brought her own two children with her. Her only duty would be the care of the children, since the Greene's employed three servants at this time.⁸⁴

While in Massachusetts Mary met and married her second husband, Henry Upham, 20 years her senior. He was a wealthy cotton merchant, married twice previously, with two teenage children. Their home in the 1870 census shows a coachman and three servants living with them.⁸⁵

Mary wasn't the only one to find marital happiness while staying with Isabella. Margaret met her husband, Russell Sturgis, Jr., while in Brookline. Like her sister Isabella, Margaret married late in life at the age of 32, and her husband had 6 children from a previous marriage. Russell was a successful merchant who hired a nurse for the children and had 4 other servants in their large home called "Sunny Waters," in Manchester, Massachusetts. "Sunny Waters was a gathering place for the family and much loved by the McCullohs." After Russell's death Margaret lived in Boston with her son James and daughter Lucy.⁸⁶

John's wife, Anna, once described her father-in-law as a man who "radiated the specific tone of the house" and inspired "awe and yet drew confidence." To

"Sunny Waters," home of Russell and Margaret Sturgis, Jr. in Manchester, Massachusetts, Courtesy of the Manchester Historical Museum.

go from that description to the symptoms of Alzheimer's was a tragic end for a man who had led such a productive life.

James died June 17, 1861. Abby died three years later on December 21, 1864. Both were buried in Greenwood Cemetery on Long Island, New York.[87]

Even though James was a lawyer, neither he nor Abby had a will. Their son John would spend many years trying to settle property issues, starting in 1849. Pennsylvania lands inherited from James' father were particularly confusing. John wrote to John Allison, whose father had been the agent living there, trying to sort out which properties remained unsold and paid $5,250 to have surveys done. Probate issues on property James owned in Maryland were still being settled at late as 1887.[88]

Chapter 7

The Civil War and Beyond

Two of James children fought for the Confederacy, while others either "avoided the war or sided with the Union." Regardless of whether they fought or not, the war had an impact on them all.

Richard McCulloh waited until his father's death before leaving New York to join the Confederacy. He submitted a letter of resignation to Columbia College, which came as a shock to his colleagues.[89] It said:

Richmond, Virginia, September 25, 1863

Gentlemen,
I hereby resign the chair I have held at Columbia College. It should encite [sic] no surprise [sic] that one, born and reared a southerner, prefers to cast his lot with that of the South. Permit me to thank you for all the generosity & consideration you have for nine years extended to me, and to assure you that I have always endeavored to justify the same, by zealous devotion to duty. I shall ever cherish the kindest remembrances of the Trustees, Faculty, & students of Columbia College & wish it prosperity & usefulness. Everything in the Physical Department will be found in order. A small a/c of Chester & Co. for acids &c. is the only outstanding bill. Apparatus ordered of M. Duboscq of Paris, will be forwarded by Samuel Haskell & Co. who have been in the habit of importing for the college.

Very truly Your Obt. Sert.
R. S. McCulloh[90]

George T. Strong, a trustee of Columbia College, commented on the surprise of Richard's resignation in his diary, "He [Richard McCulloh] has expressed no sympathy with the Rebellion and has uttered nothing worse than moderate copperheadism and he has declared himself unfavorable to slavery."[91]

Richard took with him a letter of recommendation from various professors stating he was a native of Maryland, and he expressed a desire to enter "the Confederate States [offering his] services in any way that may be useful to the Confederacy."[92] Once there he joined the Confederate Nitre and Mining Bureau in Richmond, hoping to get a commission in the Army as a chemist. This would give him protection as an officer under codes of war. When he did not receive a commission, he wrote to Confederate President Davis on July 29, 1864, expressing concern if he were captured.[93] He had reason for concern. Richard experimented with creating a lethal gas. His success came just as the war ended and before the gas could be used. He fled to Florida, but as a private citizen who had plotted against the United States, he was caught and imprisoned in the Virginia State Penitentiary in Richmond.[94]

Upon his release two years later, Robert E. Lee invited Richard to apply for the position of Professor of Natural Philosophy at Washington College—now Washington and Lee University—where Lee was President. Richard served in that capacity from 1866 to 1877. During that time, he published his "Treatise on the mechanical theory of heat and its applications to the steam-engine."[95] His last teaching position was at Louisiana State University in Baton Rouge as chair of General and Agricultural Chemistry. There he "spent eleven stormy years."[96]

Richard died at the age of 76 on 5 September 1894 while visiting his brother John at Oldfields School in Glencoe, Maryland. He was buried across the road in the Immanuel Episcopal Church Cemetery.

Oldfields was and is a girl's school started by John's wife Anna, first as a way to educate her eight children and later as a means of support after the war. John suffered from the mercantile losses of the war "which put an end to the clipper ship trade, adversely affecting" his legal practice. With failing eyesight and deteriorating health, he decided to retire.[97]

Chapter 7: The Civil War and Beyond 45

The original farmhouse at Oldfields School (with additions) in Glencoe, Maryland, Courtesy of Oldfields School

The family returned to Baltimore where Edward Austen, brother of John's wife, Anna, lent them an old farmhouse in Glencoe, 20 miles north of Baltimore. The house had 4 rooms on the first floor and 2 more floors above, with a kitchen lean-to off the dining room. When they moved in October 1867, Anna wrote in her diary:

> All the furniture is at last here and the large pieces unpacked – generally uninjured. The piano in beautiful order – the parlor glass and slab admirably put up by Jack ... No carpet will answer except as bedside pieces – I have matting that by turning I can use in the hall and parlor – indeed Duncan [her son] has tacked it down and the big bookcase is up in the hall. The dining room and its bare floors and white walls is very desolate looking, but young life soon to fill it will relieve that ... The house is a homely farmhouse – but roomy – sunshiny – clean – convenient ... The place grows on me every day.[98]

In addition to teaching her own children, Anna invited some of her nieces and nephews, as well as a few local children, most of whom were elementary age. Her two oldest daughters, Abby and Anna (called Nan), helped with the teaching, and later Caroline (called Carrie) taught drawing and painting. Within ten years the school had become a boarding school for girls with "ten resident students in addition to the McCulloh family living in the house."[99]

John lived until 1900, though "nearly totally incapacitated" by his lack of sight. The first resident nurse for the school, Lily Tilghman, helped care for him. He died at home on July 3, 1900, at the age of 83 and was buried in the Immanuel Episcopal Church Cemetery. His son Rev. Duncan McCulloch officiated the service.[100]

In her *McCulloch Chronicles*, Anna wrote about her brother-in-law William McCulloh:

"The War undid him – its expenses, its hardships, its deprivations of all his usual employments, broke up the self-control which had been so marked a feature of his young life."[101] He served in the Confederacy on the staff of

Anna (Austen) McCulloch, Courtesy of Oldfields School

Lt. Col. Henry W. Allen, future governor of Louisiana, in the 4th Infantry Regiment. This unit was organized at New Orleans in April of 1861.[102]

After the war William moved to New Orleans, living at 402 St. Andrew Street. The city directory lists him as surveyor, the census as civil engineer. Tragically, he and his wife Adeline lost another child, daughter Margie, age 2 ½. Adeline died early in 1872, at the age of 32 and he 5 years later. His son was old enough to be on his own, but his 15-year-old daughter was adopted by Margaret Cenas.[103] William's obituary describes his untimely death:

> The sudden and unexpected death of [William J. McCulloh] at the New Lake End on yesterday was a shock to his many friends in the city, as well as to the whole community. He was out bathing with a friend and while in the water was taken with a spasm. He was assisted out of the water and expired almost immediately, being afflicted with congestion of the stomach.[104]

William's twin, James W. McCulloh, and his wife became part of a group of well-to-do families forming the township of Englewood, New Jersey, at the start of the war. What had been only three farmhouses in 1859, by 1867 had a public school, street lamps, and trash removal. The Village Improvement Society planted trees, gas and water lines were laid, and the telephone arrived in 1883. James joined the baseball club and his wife, Isabella, helped form the First Presbyterian Church.[105]

Following the Civil War, Englewood struggled with thieves preying on the wealthy families residing there. The Book of Englewood said James was "a great organizer, executive and chief factor in the birth of the Protection Society." Thirty-one members were enrolled at the first meeting on January 30, 1869, with James W. McCulloh elected as president. The charter gave the society the ability to apply to the state to commission marshals and build a jail. "President McCulloh was a man of undaunted courage, never shunning dangerous service … It took grit to turn out on dark, rainy nights and do mounted patrol duty on lonely roads." In the Panic of 1873, many tramps roamed the village, due to unemployment. "The township committee proposed to President McCulloh that [the Protection Society] feed and house overnight, belated tramps. Mr.

McCulloh's reply was quite to the point: 'the entertainment of tramps, except under great emergency, is not a function of the Society, but their departure from township limits is the concern of the organization.' ... The departure of these unpleasant guests was effectively accomplished by the Society."[106]

In August of 1883 James was appointed Secretary of the Aqueduct Commission to supply water to the City of New York. His 40 years of business qualifications promoted him to the job over ten other applicants. While his services and knowledge were of "great value to the commission" when it was reorganized in 1886, the election of new commissioners greatly reduced James' salary. Some speculated this was to make him resign. He did not. Instead, James "published a letter to the citizens of New York, in which he [presented] the testimonials which secured him" the job. The *New York Times* reported that "Mr. McCulloh is better informed on the work done on the aqueduct than the Commissioners themselves." They also quoted Controller Lowe, who said, "Mr. McCulloh had been so conscientious an official that I have long felt at ease regarding any aqueduct matter that he personally vouched for as being correct." In the end it was decided James could work alongside the chief engineer for a temporary period of time.[107]

James W. McCulloh, circa 1890's

Two years later James went to Anniston, Alabama, to inspect iron interests for bondholders of the West Shore railroad. While there he suffered sunstroke, causing the loss of his eyesight. He returned to Anniston in 1893 to escape the cold of New York and, never one to sit idle, reorganized the Woodstock Iron Company. This led to becoming general manager. Even though blind, "his alert mind grasped and held information of all the innumerable little details."[108]

While in Anniston James became ill with a serious intestinal problem and died unexpectedly six weeks later. His wife, Isabella, was traveling in Europe at the time, visiting their daughter Abby, who resided in Wales.[109]

The McCulloh daughters were not as affected by the war, being married to wealthy Northerners. Having been in ill health since the birth of her second child, Isabella (McCulloh) Greene went to New York City in September of 1869 for medical treatment. Her failing health made her unable to return home to Massachusetts, so she wrote letters to her two daughters, ages 7 and 9. Her last request was to see her daughters, but before they could reach her, she died in March of 1870 at the age of 45. Isabella's funeral services were held at Trinity Church in Boston.[110]

Annie (McCulloh) Brown's daughter Susan never married and lived with her parents. The family moved to Baltimore in October of 1899 after William retired. Three months later he died suddenly of a heart attack. Annie and Susan remained at their home in Baltimore, 823 St. Paul St., until Annie's death in 1911 at the age of 81.[111]

When Adelaide's husband retired, the family moved to Philadelphia, living at 5135 Morris St. Four daughters, Mary, Jane, Anne, and Edith, lived with John and Adelaide their entire lives. Mary and her mother died within the same week in October, 1917. A newspaper account says, "Mrs. Adelaide S. Hubbard … in her eighty-sixth year and had been ill for some time. It is believed the sudden death of her daughter hastened her death."[112]

A year after Henry Upham's death in 1875, Mary and her stepdaughter traveled to Europe. She went to Europe again in 1891, 1894, and 1897 and spent summers at her house in Dublin, New Hampshire. "The last three summers she made the journey [to Dublin] in an automobile." She maintained the home in Brookline, with both of her adult stepchildren living with her, until after her stepson's death in 1882. Sometime around 1900 she moved to Boston, renting a house at 142 Marlborough Street, 4 houses from her stepdaughter and 4 blocks from her daughter Mary A. Mayer. Like her father she was community minded. "She was a member of the Sewing Circle in Boston and other social organizations. She was also a treasurer in the Associated Charities, besides having other philanthropic interest." Mary continued to employ 3 servants, 2 of whom stayed with her for over 10 years. She lived to be 95 years old, moving in with her granddaughter Belle Greene in her later years.[113]

Chapter 8

Grandchildren, a Lasting Legacy

As much as James loved family, he was probably thrilled when his first grandchild was born in 1843. Several would live with him over the years. All told he would have 49 grandchildren, 16 of whom left descendants. They are listed below, the numbers coordinating with the McCulloh lineage in the appendix.

Children of John Sears McCulloch:

23. Although born in Maryland, **George Sears McCulloch** grew up on Staten Island. He attended Columbia College in New York City, graduating in 1867. When he married Elizabeth Kip Irving five years later, his father-in-law, Rev. Pierre Paris Irving, performed the ceremony. He and his sister Abby married brother and sister. Early in their marriage George and Elizabeth lived with her parents in Castleton on Staten Island, where George was a merchant. By 1889 George and his family had moved to New Brighton on the North Shore of Staten Island, while George continued to work in Manhattan.[114]

24. **Abby Louise McCulloch** and her brother George married brother and sister. Her husband, Roland Duer Irving, attended Columbia College at the same time as her brother, which may have been how they met. Roland was already a professor of geology at Wisconsin State University when they married. Their marriage was one of the first held at the newly built Immanuel Church near Oldfields School. His early death at the age of

Immanuel Episcopal Church, built 1871-1873, near Oldfields School

41 from a stroke left Abby with a young family. In his will Roland gave everything to Abby and made her executor to his estate, but he added a note saying his wife should consult with her brother George or his cousin John Duer before making any financial decisions.[115]

After her husband's death, Abby returned to Baltimore, where she lived with her father and mother and helped teach at Oldfields School. She was "remembered as an excellent teacher of history and the history of art."[116]

25. The year before his marriage, **Duncan McCulloch** sailed for Europe. His passport describes him as 5'7", grey eyes, brown curly hair, and a beard. It is not known if this trip was for pleasure or to study for the ministry; however, he is listed as a minister at the time of his marriage to Mary Stenett Carroll, "whom he had known since she entered Oldfields [School] in 1868." Their three children attended the school.[117]

Duncan became pastor of the Immanuel Episcopal Church from the 1890s until 1913, living in the Rectory near Oldfields. Even while rector of the church, he was "available as advisor and financial manager" to his mother's school. To supplement his income as pastor, Duncan taught at

*Rev. Duncan McCulloch, age 30,
Courtesy of Oldfields School*

the school, took in boarders from the school, and raised Rhode Island Red chickens. He eventually became president of Oldfields.[118]

On 28 May 1924 Duncan and his wife sailed for Europe aboard the *Aquitania*. This time their passport said it was for pleasure and listed seven European countries they planned to visit.[119]

26. **James William McCulloch** was married twice: first to Jane Leavenworth; and second to Mary Hughes Bradley, the same year he went to work for Anson Stokes. They purchased a house at 446 Centre St., in Orange, New Jersey, where he and his family lived for the rest of their lives. In August of 1893 James became the "confidential secretary and business agent" for Anson Phelps Stokes, a wealthy New York City philanthropist. Stokes' wife described James as one "who has ever since devoted himself most faithfully and unsparingly to the interests of the family." This involved frequent travel, both in the U.S. and abroad. After Stokes' death James became the general manager of the Phelps Stokes Estate.[120] James took his own family to Europe for three months in 1923 and again in the fall of 1927.[121]

27. **John Austen McCulloch** attended his mother's school, Oldfields, in his early years. It is not known where he went to college, but he became an engineer and had a position as assistant U.S. engineer in Alleghany County, Pennsylvania. He married a Quaker woman from Baltimore, Mary Dawson Tyson Shoemaker, who had a son from a previous marriage. Their marriage only lasted 10 to 12 years, as she is found living in New Hampshire with her son in 1910, while John was still living in Pennsylvania, working as an engineer for Galeraning Works. By 1930 John was living in Denver, Colorado, as a border with no occupation.[122]

Children of Mary Louise (McCulloh) Mayer:

28. **Henry Christian Mayer** became a clergyman, and while none of the records state which denomination, his marriage leads the author to assume he was with the Episcopal Church. He lived in Newton, Massachusetts, at the beginning of his career, and in 1872 traveled to Europe with his first wife, Nina Coppee Stevens. They were visiting the seat of his Mayer ancestors in Ulm Wurtemberg when she suddenly died.[123]

    By 1880 he pastored a church in Bethlehem, Pennsylvania, eventually moving to Philadelphia, where he spent the remainder of his life. He was "prominent as a missionary and educational worker in Mexico and Cuba. His passport describes him as 5' 7", dark brown eyes, and brown hair.[124]

29. **Mary Abby Mayer's** mother was pregnant with her when her father unexpectedly died. Distraught, pregnant, and having two small children, her mother made the logical choice to move back to Washington, D.C., to live with her parents. Six months later Mary was born.

    When she was 14, Mary went with her mother to live with her Aunt Isabella's family in Newton, Massachusetts. Her mother was to care for her aunt's infant daughter while her aunt went to Europe for the health of her husband. Mary spent the next year living in the same household with a cousin by marriage, J. S. Copley Greene, Jr. who, 7 years later, became her husband.[125]

Copley attended Harvard but dropped out in his junior year. "In 1867 he went to Europe, returning in September, and entered Harvard Medical School." Having sown his wild oats, he must have been ready to settle down, because Mary and Copley married the following year. They spent the summer honeymooning in Switzerland. When he graduated in March of 1871, he and Mary again went to Europe, this time with their 6-month-old-baby. Copley died at the age of 27 while they were in Berlin. Perhaps he had health issues, because he made out his will several months before his marriage.[126]

In a situation much like her mother's, Mary found herself pregnant, with a young child and the loss of her husband. She remained in Europe for at least another month until her son Henry was born November 21, 1871, in Vienna. Upon her return to the States, Mary lived in Philadelphia for a few years. She later moved back to Boston, living at 354 Marlborough St., and when the children were older, she took them to Europe in 1884, 1891, 1894, and 1897.[127]

Children of William James McCulloh:

30. **Richard McCall McCulloh** attended Virginia Military Institute in Lexington, Virginia, and then studied law at the University of Louisiana. That may be where he met his future wife, Bertha M. Bercegeay, whose father, Augustin Bercegeay, was a professor. Richard was admitted to the Louisiana bar in 1880, and a year later he and Bertha were married. He practiced law for eight years until he was elected as district attorney for Ascension Parish and also served as Superintendent of Schools.[128]

    "During the war with Spain in 1898, Captain McCulloh organized a company of artillery known as the Donaldsonville Cannoneers … stationed at Jackson Barracks in New Orleans." He was mustered in on July 7, 1898.[129]

    From 1908 until his death, Richard represented the Ninth District in the Louisiana State Senate. His obituary describes his unexpected death:

    > He was apparently in the best of health about 5 o'clock attending to business matters with his law partner, B. J. Vega… About 5:15

o'clock Captain McCulloh went to his residence, complaining of violent pain. Mrs. McCulloh left the room to prepare some medicine for him, when she returned, not more than five minutes later, the senator was struggling for breath, and she then called Mr. Vega. Before medical assistance could reach him he was dead. Drs. John D. Hanson and E. K. Sims stated that death was in all probability caused by heart failure.[130]

31. **Abby Sears McCulloh**'s mother died when she was 7, her father when she was 12. She was adopted and raised by Margaret Cenas, a friend of the family. Abby and her husband, Emile J. Delvaille, purchased a house sometime between 1900 and 1910 at 1433 N. Robertson St. in New Orleans. After his early death Abby continued to live there with her daughter Anita, also widowed young, until her own death in 1936.[131]

Children of James William McCulloh:

32. **Caroline McCulloh** and her husband, William Lemmon, raised their family in Englewood, New Jersey, where Caroline had grown up. William was a stockbroker, most likely working in New York City. Sometime between 1920 and 1930, William and Caroline moved to Marietta, Georgia, which could have been for retirement or to be closer to their son William and his family. After William's death Caroline lived with their unmarried daughter, Mary, until Mary's death. From there it appears she went to live with her son George in Birmingham, Alabama, for the last two years of her life.[132]

33. **Charles Sears McCulloh** became a successful New York City accountant with a reputation for honesty. He was one of the first public accountants in Manhattan and joined the firm of Haskins and Sells in 1898, eventually making partner. After practicing on his own for a time, he joined the firm of F. W. Lafrentz & Co, where "for seventeen years Charles was chief examiner for the State of New York."[133]

He courted his future wife, Kate Monteath Mayo, for 9 years before marrying her. Early in their marriage they rented an apartment at 206

West 69th St. in Manhattan. They later purchased what we would today call a condominium at 223 W. 139th St., where they lived for the next 15 years. After his second marriage, Charles moved to 1105 Park Ave. and bought a summer home in Florida near Miami on Sunset Island No. 1.[134]

Charles loved sailing and was a member of the Cherry Diamond Yacht Club, serving as treasurer in 1892. He owned 2 different yachts (a 50-footer and later a 70-footer) on which they spent summer vacations sailing around Long Island Sound. He also had a small sailboat moored in Flushing Bay that was used regularly.[135]

In addition to sailing, Charles was an avid bicyclist. An interesting article in the *New York Tribune* describes a parade in 1896:

> The parade last night held under the auspices of the McKinley and Hobart Wheelmen's League was inspiring. Many prominent wheelmen were in line ... and it is said that almost every member of this club is a Republican ... The alignment of the parade on its long journey through the streets was excellent all the way to the reviewing stand at Madison-ave. and Twenty-sixth-st. The marshal's aids were experienced cyclists who had acted in that capacity at other bicycle parades and they handled their charges like well-drilled soldiers.
>
> The McKinley League, which is composed of 2000 enrolled riders had the right of line. Following them came the New-York Republican Bicycle Brigade, numbering 300. The Sound Money Club Wheelmen of Tarrytown came next numbering nearly 400 and bringing up the rear there were possibly 1000 unattached wheelmen and wheelwomen. The marshal's aids and officials wore white uniforms with blue and gold trimmings and golf stockings. On their heads they wore gilded helmets, some of which had pictures of McKinley on the front and others being decorated with a golden eagle ... Marshal of Third Division, John B. Yates. Aids – Peter Burkhart, Charles S. McCulloh and George G. Cook.[136]

Charles walked to work every day. At 80 he was healthy and going strong until he fell on some ice and broke his hip. From there it was a downward struggle, and after a 2-year illness, he died while at his Miami Beach home.[137]

34. **Allan McCulloh** attended law school at Columbia College, graduating in 1878, and became a lawyer in New York City. He moved to Manhattan sometime after 1900 with his mother and sister Mary. He and his sister would live together for the next 20 years. He became a senior member of the firm Alexandar and Green and vice president of the Bar of the City of New York.[138]

Allan traveled to Europe almost every other year between 1889 and 1931. He must have been interested in his family history, because he was involved in the St. Andrew's Society, the Sons of the Revolution, and the Society of Colonial Wars. He never married.[139]

35. **Robert Lee McCulloh's** second marriage to Eleanor Bell in 1899 listed him as living in Punxsutawney, Pennsylvania, his occupation as civil engineer. The 1910 census shows them living in Greensburg, Pennsylvania, where he was a construction supervisor for the railroad. They may have moved to Canada, or perhaps they were visiting there for Christmas, when Robert died suddenly of heart problems. No record of children was found for either of his marriages.[140]

36. **Walter McCulloh** was a civil engineer, living most of his life in Niagara Falls. The year he married he was involved with the construction of a single-arch bridge across the Niagara Gorge near Niagara Falls. He assisted the construction engineer, R.S. Buck, by "supervising the construction of masonry." At the time this was the longest single-arch bridge in the world. For a short period from about 1910 to 1911, he lived in Albany, where he was the "consulting engineer of the New York State Water Supply Commission." He returned to Niagara Falls and there purchased a home at 319 Jefferson Ave., where he and his wife, Caroline Wright, lived until their deaths. Walter was written up in *Who's Who in New York* for his

Chapter 8: Grandchildren, a Lasting Legacy   59

International Upper Steel Arch Bridge, 1905-1920, Detroit Publishing Co., Library of Congress

construction work, particularly, two suspension bridges over the Niagara River. Walter and Caroline adopted a little girl. Their daughter, Dorothy, and her family moved in with Walter sometime around 1940 and continued living there after Walter's death.[141]

37. **James Sears McCulloh** lived the American dream. He started out a clerk for the West Shore Railroad, making $3 a week, and ended up a President of the New York Telephone Company. His early interest in communications let him to the operating headquarters of the railroad and the Western Union Telegraph Company in Weehawken, New Jersey. There for three years "he studied telephone and telegraph operations, wire testing, line construction and maintenance."[142]

This was a time of major growth for the young telephone industry. American Telephone and Telegraph Company (AT&T) was formed in 1885 as part of the Bell system. They opened a long distance line in 1892, connecting New York City with Chicago. When Alexander Graham

Warriston" home of James Sear McCulloh in Rye, New York, 1906

Bell's second patent expired in 1894, over 6,000 independent telephone companies jumped into the market.[143]

In 1898 James married Sarah May Gause, a divorced woman with one daughter. He adopted her ten-year-old daughter, Mildred, shortly after they were married, and a year later they had a son of their own.

The year after AT&T initiated their long distance line, James connected with AT&T, becoming their "chief operator of the department in New York." "In 1901 he was sent to Chicago as superintendent of the American Telephone and Telegraph Co.'s midwest division." James returned to New York in 1904 to be superintendent of buildings and supplies for New York Telephone, which was one-seventh of the entire Bell system at this point. He was appointed vice president of "public relations and commercial work from 1919 to 1923." A few months later he became president of the company.[144]

"During his years as president, the company underwent a period of vast transition and expansion. The first dial telephone was installed in the city just two years before he became head of the company." James retired in 1933 but remained a member of the board until 1938.[145]

Like his grandfather he was active in the community. He was a member of the American Yacht Club, founder of the Manursing Island Club, and "once served as chairman of the New York State Chamber of Commerce. James served as treasurer of the Apawamis Club and of the Rye

Presbyterian Church ... [belonged] to the St. Andrew's Society of New York State and [was] a member of the Railroad Club of New York City."[146]

Sometime before 1910 James bought a house at 890 Forest Ave. in Rye. Early on he employed several servants, including a groom and coachman. By 1915 he had switched to the use of an automobile, employing a chauffeur.[147]

38. **Abby Sears McCulloh** was the youngest daughter of James W. and Isabella McCulloh. She traveled to England with her mother in 1894 when she was 24. It is not known if she met her future husband, Arthur Lloyd Roberts, while traveling in Europe or if they met in New York, since he had been to New York in 1893 and 1894. Born in Liverpool, England, Arthur came from a wealthy family and, after graduating from Cambridge University, joined the family business as a timber merchant. They were married in Englewood, New Jersey, on January 12, 1896. Abby may have remained in New Jersey with her family for the next year, because Arthur crossed the Atlantic three times by himself in 1896. Abby and her mother had returned to England in 1897 when her father died.[148]

By 1901 Abby and Arthur were living in Wales with Arthur's brother's family in Denbighshire, Wales. Abby returned to New York to visit her family in 1903, 1908, and 1911. The 1911 England census shows them living in Heswall, Cheshire County. They had no children.[149]

Children of Adelaide (McCulloh) Hubbard:

39. **Russell Sturgis Hubbard** was a banker in Philadelphia, working for the Finance Company of Pennsylvania. By 1904 he had moved up to 1st Vice President and Treasurer of Harrison Bros. & Co., a manufacturer of paint.[150]

40. After her marriage, **Lucy Sturgis Hubbard** and her husband, William H. Jefferys, lived with his parents in Philadelphia. William was a physician. Sometime after 1900 Lucy and William went to live in China, where daughters Lucy and Adelaide were born. They returned home in December of 1911 before moving to London, England, where he is listed as a surgeon. He set up private practice in Philadelphia around 1916.[151]

Children of Margaret (McCulloh) Sturgis:

41. After graduating from Harvard University in 1890, **Sullivan Warren Sturgis** took a one-year tour of Europe with his twin brother, Edward. Upon returning, Sullivan, who went by the name of S. Warren, taught Latin at Groton School in Groton, Massachusetts. He married Edith Barnes in 1899. Sometime before 1920 he must have inherited money, because the census index shows him still teaching at Groton but living in Boston with seven servants.[152]

    Sullivan took his oldest son, Somers, to England and France in 1922, and his son Warren and daughter Edith to Europe the following year. He continued to teach at Groton School until retiring, when he moved permanently to Boston, living at 66 Marlborough Street.[153]

42. **Edward Sturgis** and his brother were twins. Since Edward was 5' 11" and Sullivan, was 6' 1", they could not have been identical. Like his brother, Edward graduated from Harvard and went with Sullivan on a one-year tour of Europe. This must have made a positive impression because, after marrying Josephine Putnam in 1902, they honeymooned in England. The ship's manifest lists him as clergyman. In March of 1903 Edward and Josephine returned to Europe to live in Lucerne, Switzerland, for two years, where their first two sons were born.[154]

    Why he left the ministry is not known, but the 1910 census finds Edward living in Andover, Massachusetts, as a farmer, with four servants in the household. Also confusing is why he left this farm, which he owned, to rent a house in Milton, Massachusetts, for the rest of his life. He died there in 1939.[155]

43. **James McCulloh Sturgis** attended Harvard, graduating in 1896. He never married, lived with his mother and sister, and had a career in advertising. During World War I he served in France with the Y.M.C.A. He "served in [the] Cinema Department, Paris [from] October 1917 to May 1918" and was then "appointed director of Foyer du Soldat, Faux-Saint-Pierre, with [the] Army of Occupation" in Germany from December 1918 to February 1920.[156]

Chapter 9

The British Connection

Because people who read this book may have a connection to the British McCullohs, a decision was made to include a little about them, even though they did not have any direct impact on the life of James W. McCulloh.

Robert McCulloh, the oldest brother of John McCulloh, James W.'s father, lived in England, working as a barrister in London. Family lore says that Robert came to America with Lord Cornwallis during the American Revolution and there met his second wife, Frances Roupell. Frances' brother George was a "searcher of customs" for the city of Charleston, and being loyalists, they both fled to England in 1782. This is where the two families became intertwined. George Roupell's son, George Boone Roupell, married Robert's daughter, Frances, by his first wife.[157]

Despite the brothers fighting on opposite sides during the Revolution, it does not appear to have severed the family connections. Years after the war James W.'s oldest brother, Samuel, went to England to marry his cousin Eleanor McCulloh, Robert's youngest daughter. They returned to the United States to live at his plantation, Rockland, in Maryland. Thus began a tie between the British and American McCullohs that would last for several generations.[158]

Letters crossed the Atlantic for over 50 years, beginning before Robert's death in 1789. Aunts and uncles kept their nieces and nephews abreast of family happenings. Eleanor, of course, would have wanted to stay in touch with her sister in England. When she died Samuel had her remains shipped to England to be buried in the family vault at Charlton, County Kent.[159]

With the death of Eleanor, known letters to England stop, but the numerous trips to Europe by future family members makes one wonder if contact continued. James W.'s daughter Mary Louisa went to England in 1876 after the death of her husband. She then returned with her daughter Mary (Mayer) Greene and grandchildren in 1891, 1894, and 1897. Granddaughter Abby (McCulloh) Roberts lived in England after meeting and marrying an Englishman. Grandson Allan McCulloh went to Europe almost every other year between 1889 and 1931.[160]

Appendix

McCulloh Family Lineage

1. **John¹ McCulloh**, b. 1721 in Belfast, Ireland, son of Robert. He married **Elizabeth McBlair**.[161] She married second _____ Rankin, d. abt. June 1792.[162]

   Children of John and Elizabeth (McBlair) McCulloh:
   2. i. Robert² McCulloh, b. 17 Sept. 1742,[163] c. 10 April 1743, Barr by Girvan, ii William² McCulloh, c. 14 July 1747, Barr by Girvan, Ayr.[165]
   3. iii. William² McCulloh, c. 4 November 1748, Barr by Girvan, Ayr.[166]
   4. iv. John² McCulloh (II), b. 20 April 1747, c. 23 September 1750, Barr by Girvan, Ayr.[167]
   5. v. James² McCulloh, c. 1 February 1754, Barr by Girvan, Ayr.[168]
   6. vi. Sarah² McCulloh, c. 16 May, 1761, Dailly, Ayr, Scotland.[169]
   7. vii. Anne² McCulloh, c. 20 July 1765, Dailly, Ayr.[170]
   viii. Joseph² McCulloh.[171]
   ix. Samuel² McCulloh.[172]

2. **Robert² McCulloh** (*John¹*), b. 17 Sept. 1742, d. 27 May 1789, Charlton, Kent, England.[173] He married first **Frances Browne**,[174] married second **Frances Roupell**, sister of George Boone Roupell.[175]

Children of Robert and Frances (Browne) McCulloh:
- ii. Frances³ McCulloh, b. between 1770-1772, d. 8 Feb. 1853, Greenwich, London, England.[176]
- i. Eleanor³ McCulloh.[177]
- iii. Francis³ McCulloh, b. 1770, d. 1 April 1816, Greenwich, London.[178]

3. **William² McCulloh** (*John¹*), c. 4 November, 1748, d. 22 March 1783, Philadelphia, Pennsylvania.[179] He married 3 June 1772 in Philadelphia, **Hannah Williams**.[180]

Child of William and Hannah (Williams) McCulloh:
- i. Margaret³ McCulloh, d. 27 March 1784.[181]

4. **John² McCulloh (II)** (*John¹*), b. 20 April 1747 in Kirkcudbright, Scotland,[182] d. 13 April 1800 in Philadelphia, Pennsylvania, and is buried in the churchyard of the Old Pine Street Church on the corner of Pine and 4th Streets.[183] He married first in Philadelphia, 19 April 1771, to **Anna Todd**,[184] born 1747 in Philadelphia, the daughter of Andrew and Elizabeth (McDowell) Todd.[185] She died February 19, 1789. He married second in Philadelphia, 8 April 1790, **Anna Bringhurst**,[186] b. 28 November 1859,[187] daughter of John and Elizabeth (Shute) Bringhurst,[188] d. 28 May 1848 in Philadelphia.[189]

Children of John and Anna (Todd) McCulloh, all born in Philadelphia:[190]
- 8. i. Samuel³ McCulloh, b. 20 January 1772.
- ii. Andrew³ McCulloh, b. 18 July 1774, d. 6 August 1809 in New Orleans, Louisiana.[191]
- iii. Elizabeth³ McCulloh, b. 4 November 1776.
- iv. Anne³ McCulloh, b. 8 June 1779, d. 17 March 1798.[192]
- 9. v. Mary³ McCulloh, b. 30 March 1782.
- vi. John³ McCulloh, b. 27 October 1784, d. 28 June 1806.[193]
- 10. vii. Margaret³ McCulloh, b. 19 January 1787.
- 11. viii. James³ William Benoi Todd McCulloh, b. 5 February 1789.

Children of John and Anna (Bringhurst) McCulloh, all born in Philadelphia:[194]
  ix. George[3] Bringhurst McCulloh, b. 30 January 1791.
  x. Sarah[3] Bringhurst McCulloh, b. 20 April 1792, d. 28 May 1867 in New Jersey.[195]
12. xi. Isabella[3] Williamson McCulloh, b. 18 August 1793.
  xii. Robert[3] Pierce McCulloh, b. 10 February 1795.
  xiii. Isaac[3] Bringhurst McCulloh, b. 9 November 1796, d. 9 November 1815.[196]
  xiv. Eleanor[3] McCulloh, b. 15 January 1798.
  xv. Anne[3] Smith McCulloh, b. 31 July 1799, d. 13 August 1853 in Philadelphia.[197]
13. xvi. William[3] Shute McCulloh, b. 7 January 1800.

5. **James**[2] **McCulloh** (*John*[1]), c. 1 February 1754, d. 8 January 1798 in Baltimore, Maryland.[198] He married **Peggy** _____.[199]

6. **Sarah**[2] **McCulloh** (*John*[1]), c. 16 May, 1761. She married **Edward Pannell**.[200]

Children of Edward and Sarah (McCulloh) Pannell, all born in Baltimore:[201]
  i. James[3] Pannell, b. 21 May 1784.
  ii. Hugh[3] Pannell, b. 11 April 1785.
  iii. William[3] Pannell, b. 18 June 1788.
  iv. Elizabeth[3] Pannell, b. 13 August 1791.
  v. Edward[3] Pannell, b. 10 January 1794.
  vi. George[3] Washington Pannell, b. 18 March 1796
  vii. Ann[3] Pierce Pannell, b. 18 January 1800
  viii. Jane[3] Pannell
  ix. Sarah[3] McCulloh Pannell

7. **Anne**[2] **McCulloh** (*John*[1]), c. 20 July 1765, d. 20 April 1786.[202] She married in Philadelphia, 31 August 1773, **David Williamson**.[203]

Children of David and Ann (McCulloh) Williamson:
  i. Isabella[3] Williamson, married in Boston, 10 July 1803, Samuel McCulloh.
  ii. Mary Elizabeth[3] Williamson, married in Baltimore, 10 Aug. 1798, Levi Pierce.[204]
  iii. Anna Williamson, married in Baltimore, 6 Aug. 1789, Humphrey Pierce.[205]

8. **Samuel**[3] **McCulloh** (*John*[2], *John*[1]), b. 20 January 1772, d. 30 December 1848 in Baltimore.[206] He married first in Boston, 10 July 1803, his cousin, **Isabella Williamson**.[207] He married second in Durham, England, 5 August 1824, his cousin, **Eleanor McCulloh**.[208]

Children of Samuel and Isabella (Williamson) McCulloh:[209]
  i. Anne Eliza McCulloh, married 30 June 1836 in Baltimore, Jacob Green.[210]
  ii. Samuel McCulloh.

9. **Mary**[3] **McCulloh** (*John*[2], *John*[1]), b. 30 March 1782, d. 23 November 1817.[211] She married 3 October 1815 in Philadelphia, **Rev. Ashbel Green**, the eighth president of the College of New Jersey and co-founder of the Princeton Theological Seminary.[212]

10. **Margaret**[3] **McCulloh** (*John*[2], *John*[1]), b. 19 January 1787, d. 3 December 1852 in Muscatine, Iowa.[213] She married **Charles Cummins**.[214]

11. **James**[3] **William Benoi Todd McCulloh** (*John*[2], *John*[1]), b. 5 February 1789 in Philadelphia,[215] d. 17 June 1861, in Orange, New Jersey.[216] He married in Baltimore, 19 May 1814, **Abigail Sears**,[217] b. 19 May 1797 in Newport, Rhode Island, dau. of George and Lucrecia (Fry) Sears,[218] d. 21 December 1864, in Orange, New Jersey.[219]

Children of James W. and Abby (Sears) McCulloh, all born in Baltimore:[220]
14. i. John[4] Sears McCulloch, b. 28 November 1816.[221]

Appendix: McCulloh Family Lineage 69

15. ii. Richard⁴ Sears McCulloh, b. 18 March 1818.²²²
16. iii. Mary⁴ Louisa McCulloh, b. 20 October 1821²²³
    iv. Elizabeth⁴ Ann McCulloh, b. 11 May 1822, d. 1824
17. v. Isabella⁴ Williamson McCulloh, b. 1 May 1825.²²⁴
18. vi. William⁴ James McCulloh, twin of James W., b. 19 March 1827.²²⁵
19. vii. James⁴ William McCulloh, twin of William J., b. 19 March 1827.
20. viii. Annie⁴ Lucretia McCulloh, b. 27 September 1829.²²⁶
21. ix. Adelaide⁴ Sears McCulloh, b. 10 December 1831.²²⁷
22. x. Margaret⁴ McCulloh, b. 19 January 1834.²²⁸

12. **Isabella³ Williamson McCulloh** (*John²*, *John¹*), b. 18 August 1793, d. 11 March 1865, in Philadelphia.²²⁹ She married 25 January 1825 in New Jersey, **James Sprout Green**, son of Rev. Ashbel Green.²³⁰

Children of James S. and Isabella (McCulloh) Green, all born in Princeton, New Jersey:
    i. Ashbel⁴ Green, b. 17 December 1825.²³¹
    ii. Anna⁴ Green, b. 22 May 1827.²³²
    iii. James⁴ Sprout Green, Jr., b. 22 July 1829.²³³
    iv. Robert⁴ Stockton Green, b. 25 March 1831, became the 35ᵗʰ Governor of New Jersey.²³⁴
    v. Isabella⁴ W. Green, b. 25 January 1834.²³⁵

13. **William³ Shute McCulloh** (*John²*, *John¹*), b. 7 January 1800, d. before Nov. 1850, in Baltimore.²³⁶ He married **Galatee Labordaire**.²³⁷

Children of William S. and Galatee (Labordaire) McCulloh:²³⁸
    i. George⁴ McCulloh.
    ii. Josephine⁴ McCulloh.
    iii. Chlorine⁴ McCulloh.
    iv. Isabelle⁴ McCulloh.

14. **John⁴ Sears McCulloch** (*James³*, *John²*, *John¹*), b. 28 November 1816, d. 3 July 1900, buried Immanuel Episcopal Church Cemetery in Glencoe,

Maryland.²³⁹ He married at the Associate Reformed Church in Baltimore, 31 October 1844, **Anna Austen**.²⁴⁰ She was born 10 October 1823, in Baltimore, the daughter of George Austen, II and Caroline Millemon,²⁴¹ d. 26 March 1904, buried Immanuel Cemetery, Glencoe.²⁴²

Children of John² Sears and Anna (Austen) McCulloch:
23. i. George⁵ Sears McCulloch, b. 31 July 1845, in Baltimore.²⁴³
24. ii. Abby⁵ Louise McCulloch, b. 28 February 1847, in Baltimore.²⁴⁴
    iii. Anna⁵ Green McCulloch, b. 9 December 1848, in New York, d. 1 March 1928, in Glencoe.²⁴⁵
    iv. Caroline⁵ Austen McCulloch, b. 20 September 1851, in Southfield, New York, d. 4 November 1898, in Glencoe.²⁴⁶
25. v. Duncan⁵ McCulloch, b. 15 September 1853, on Staten Island.²⁴⁷
    vi. Edward⁵ Austen McCulloch, b. 15 November 1856, on Staten Island,²⁴⁸ d. 1932 in Springfield State [Mental] Hospital, Carrol County, Maryland.²⁴⁹
26. vii. James⁵ William McCulloch, b. 9 October 1857, Richmond Co., New York.²⁵⁰
    viii. Alice⁵ McCulloch, twin, b. 1861 on Staten Island, d. 1861.²⁵¹
    x. Margie⁵ McCulloch, twin, b. 1861 on Staten Island, d. 1861.²⁵²
27. xi. John⁵ Austen McCulloch, b. July 1864 on Staten Island.²⁵³

15. Richard⁴ Sears McCulloh (*James³, John², John¹*), b. 18 March 1818, in Baltimore, d. 5 September 1894 in Maryland and is buried in the Immanuel Episcopal Church Cemetery in Glencoe.²⁵⁴ He married **Mary Stewart Vowell**.²⁵⁵

Child of Richard² Sears and Mary (Vowell) McCulloh:
   i. Margaretta⁵ Grace McCulloh, b. 4 April 1847, d. 1 Sept. 1921.²⁵⁶

16. Mary⁴ Louisa McCulloh (*James³, John², John¹*), b. 21 October 1821, in Baltimore, d. 30 November 1916, in Boston.²⁵⁷ She married first in Baltimore on 4 May 1842, **Henry Christian Mayer**,²⁵⁸ b. 5 May 1821, son of Charles F. Mayer, d. 1 March 1846, in Rochester, New York.²⁵⁹

Appendix: McCulloh Family Lineage

Gravestones of John S. and Anna (Austen) McCulloch, Immanuel Episcopal Church Cemetery

She married second in Natick, Massachusetts, on 4 June 1861, **Henry Upham**,[260] born about 1800 in Brookline, Massachusetts, d. 25 April 1875 in Brookline.[261]

Children of Henry and Mary² Louisa (McCulloh) Mayer:
    i.   Susan⁵ Theresa Mayer, b. 19 February 1843 in Baltimore,[262] d. 18 February 1857 in New York.[263]
28. ii.   Henry⁵ Christian Mayer, b. 3 March 1844 in New York[264]
    iii. Frederick⁵ Melchior Mayer, b. 21 July 1845, d. 21 November 1845.[265]
29. iv. Mary⁵ Abby Mayer, b. 14 September 1846 in Washington, D.C.[266]

17. **Isabella⁴ Williamson McCulloh** (*James³, John², John¹*), b. 1 May 1825 in Baltimore, d. 15 March 1870 in New York City.[267] She married in Massachusetts about 1858, **Rev. John Singleton Copley Greene**,[268] b. 1811, d. 6 July 1872 in Brookline.[269]

Children of Rev. J. S. Copley and Isabella⁴ (McCulloh) Greene:
    i.   Mary⁵ Emery Greene, b. 3 May 1860 in Newton, Mass.[270]
    ii.   Margaret⁵ Greene, b. 11 February 1862.[271]

18. William⁴ James McCulloh (*James³, John², John¹*), b. 19 March 1827 in Baltimore, twin of James William McCulloh, d. 15 August 1877 in New Orleans, Louisiana.[272] He married in Ascension Parish, Louisiana, on 24 March 1856, **Adeline E. Bercegeay**,[273] born about 1840 in Louisiana, daughter of Alphonse and Elizabeth Bercegeay.[274]

Children of William⁴ James and Adeline (Bercegeay) McCulloh:
        i.   James⁵ McCulloh, b. 1857 in Donaldsonville.[275]
30. ii.   Richard⁵ McCall McCulloh, b. February 1858 in Donaldsonville.[276]
        iii. Unnamed boy, b. 1860 in Donaldsonville.[277]
31. iv. Abby⁵ Sears McCulloh, b. 27 February 1865 in Donaldsonville.[278]
        v.   Margie⁵ McCulloh, b. 1867, d. 11 April 1870 in New Orleans.[279]

19. James⁴ William McCulloh (*James³, John², John¹*), b. 19 March 1827 in Baltimore, twin of William James, d. 3 May 1897 in Anniston, Alabama.[280] He married in New York City on 19 December 1850, **Isabella Steel Walker**,[281] born 27 June 1929 in New York City, daughter of William and Caroline Lydia (Steel) Walker.[282]

Children of James⁴ W. and Isabella (Walker) McCulloh:
32. i.   Caroline⁵ McCulloh, b. 16 February 1852, New York City.[283]
        ii.   Henry⁵ Mayer McCulloh, b. 24 December 1853, New York City,[284] d. bef. 1860.[285]
33. iii. Charles⁵ Sears McCulloh, b. 1 July 1856, Riverdale, Westchester, NY.[286]
34. iv. Allan⁵ McCulloh, b. 27 September 1858, Ossining, New York.[287]
35. v.   Robert⁵ Lee McCulloh, b. 31 August 1860, Ossining, New York.[288]
36. vi. Walter⁵ McCulloh, b. 24 October 1862, Ossining, New York.[289]
        vii. Archy⁵ McCulloh, b. 12 January 1865, Englewood, New Jersey, d. 20 April 1932 in Manhattan.[290]
        viii. Mary⁵ Eaton McCulloh, b. 16 May 1866, Englewood,[291] d. 17

October 1934 in Manhattan.[292]
37. ix. James[5] Sears McCulloh, b. 5 September 1868, Englewood.[293]
38. x. Abby[5] Sears McCulloh, b. 8 March 1870, Englewood.[294]
   xi. Lewis[5] Spencer McCulloh, b. 24 February 1874, Englewood,[295] d. Aug. 1877.[296]

20. **Annie**[4] **Lucretia McCulloh** (*James*[3], *John*[2], *John*[1]), b. 27 September 1829 in Baltimore, d. 7 March 1911 in Baltimore.[297] She married in Washington, D.C., on 6 June 1853, **William Isaac Brown**,[298] born 14 January 1825, died 4 January 1900.[299]

   Children of William and Annie[4] (McCulloh) Brown:
   i. William[5] McCulloh Brown, b. 13 November 1854, d. 14 December 1936.[300]
   ii. Susan[5] Theresa Brown, b. 11 July 1862, d. 27 April 1944.[301]

21. **Adelaide**[4] **Sears McCulloh** (*James*[3], *John*[2], *John*[1]), b. 10 December 1831 in Baltimore,[302] d. 13 October 1917 in Philadelphia.[303] She married in Washington, D.C. on 27 June 1849, **Rev. John P. Hubbard**.[304]

   Children of John P. and Adelaide[4] (McCulloh) Hubbard:
   i. Mary[5] Hubbard, b. 1851, Virginia.
   ii. Jane[5] (Jennie) Hubbard, b. 28 Feb. 1852, Worthington, Massachusetts, d. 25 February 1904, Philadelphia.[305]
   iii. John[5] P. Hubbard, b. 7 August 1853, Northampton, Massachusetts.[306]
   iv. Margaret[5] Hubbard, b. 1854, Northampton,[307] d. 18 May 1857.[308]
   v. John[5] Parkinson Hubbard, b. 3 July 1860, Westerly, Rhode Island.[309]
39. vi. Russell[5] Sturgis Hubbard, b. 2 June 1863, Westerly.[310]
   vii. Ann[5] McCulloh Hubbard, b. 6 September 1866, Westerly, d. 15 October 1927, Philadelphia.[311]
   viii. William[5] Hubbard, b. 19 March 1868, Westerly,[312] d. before 1870.[313]
40. ix. Lucy[5] Sturgis Hubbard, b. 19 July 1872, Massachusetts.[314]
   x. Edith[5] Hubbard, b. 4 August 1874, West Virginia, d. 7 January 1923, Philadelphia.[315]

22. **Margaret**[4] **McCulloh** (*James*[3], *John*[2], *John*[1]), was born 19 January 1834 in Baltimore, d. 25 November 1927 in Manchester, Massachusetts. She married in Brookline, Massachusetts, on 29 May 1866, **Russell Sturgis, Jr.**

Children of Russell and Margaret[4] (McCulloh) Sturgis:
- 41. i. Sullivan[5] Warren Sturgis, twin of Edward, b. 24 April 1868, Boston.[316]
- 42. ii. Edward[5] Sturgis, twin of Sullivan b. 24 April 1868, Boston.
- 43. iii. James[5] McCulloh Sturgis, b. 13 November 1872, Boston.[317]
- iv. Lucy[5] Codman Sturgis, b. 11 February 1876, Brookline.[318]

23. **George**[5] **Sears McCulloch** (*John*[4], *James*[3], *John*[2], *John*[1]), b. 31 July 1845 in Baltimore, d. 16 August 1925 in New York City, buried in Sleepy Hollow Cemetery, Bronx, New York.[319] He married at Christ Church, New Brighton, New York on 12 June 1873, **Elizabeth Kip Irving**.[320] She was born 12 April 1835 in Geneva, New York, daughter of Rev. Pierre Paris and Anna Katharine (Duer) Irving.[321]

Child of George[5] and Elizabeth (Irving) McCulloch:
- i. Robert[6] Austen McCulloch, b. 23 August 1874 in New York.[322]

24. **Abby**[5] **Louise McCulloch** (*John*[4], *James*[3], *John*[2], *John*[1]), b. 28 February 1847 in Baltimore, d. 20 October 1905 in Baltimore.[323] She married at St. James Protestant Episcopal Church in Baltimore, on 8 August 1872, **Roland Duer Irving**,[324] born 27 April 1847 in New York City, the son of Rev. Pierre P. and Ann (Duer) Irving,[325] d. 30 May 1888.[326]

Children of Roland D. and Abby[5] L. (McCulloch) Irving, all born in Madison, Wisconsin:
- i. Anna[6] Duer Irving, b. April 1873.
- ii. John[6] Duer Irving, b. 1874.
- iii. Peter[6] Irving, b. 3 Aug 1878.[327]
- iv. Pierre[6] Frederick Irving, b. 1880.

25. Rev. Duncan⁵ McCulloch (*John⁴, James³, John², John¹*), b. 15 September 1853 on Staten Island, d. 20 November 1932 in Glencoe, Maryland.³²⁸ He married on 29 December 1897, **Mary Stenett Carroll,** born 1 July 1861, daughter of Henry and Mary (Winchester) Carroll.³²⁹

Children of Duncan⁵ and Mary (Carroll) McCulloch, all born in Baltimore:
  i.   Mary⁶ Winchester Carroll McCulloch, b. 1 November 1889.³³⁰
  ii. Duncan⁶ McCulloch, b. 14 September 1898.³³¹
  iii. Anna⁶ Austen McCulloch, b. 30 July 1903.³³²

26. James⁵ William McCulloch (*John⁴, James³, John², John¹*), b. 9 October 1857 in Richmond Co, New York, d. 1938 in Orange, New Jersey, buried at Rosedale Cemetery in Orange.³³³ He married first at St. Stephens Episcopal Church in Wilkes Barre, Pennsylvania, on 28 January 1886, **Jane Leavenworth,** born 1855 in Wilkes Barre, daughter of Franklin and Eunice Leavenworth.³³⁴ She died 26 February 1887 in Brooklyn, New York, five days after the birth of her son.³³⁵ James married second in Washington, DC, on 11 April 1893, **Mary Hughes Bradley**, born 1865 in Montgomery, Maryland.³³⁶

Child of James⁵ W. and Jane (Leavenworth) McCulloch:
  i. Paul⁶ Leavenworth McCulloch, b. 21 February 1887 in Wilkes Barre.³³⁷

Children of James⁵ W. and Mary (Bradley) McCulloch, all born in Orange:
  ii. Duncan⁶ Bradley McCulloch, stillborn, 13 January 1893.³³⁸
  iii. Elizabeth⁶ Duncan McCulloch, b. 23 January 1895.³³⁹
  iv. Warren⁶ Sturgis McCulloch, b. 6 November 1899.³⁴⁰
  v. Margaret⁶ Callender McCulloch, b. 16 January 1901.³⁴¹

27. John⁵ Austen McCulloch (*John⁴, James³, John², John¹*), b. July 1864 on Staten Island, New York, d. 1938 in Denver, Colorado, buried in Immanuel Cemetery in Glencoe, Maryland.³⁴² He married in Baltimore, about 1898, **Mary Dawson (Tyson) Shoemaker**, born 9 December 1866, daughter of

James W. and Elizabeth W. Tyson,[343] d. 24 August 1926, Orange County, Vermont, buried in Evergreen Cemetery.[344] No known children.

28. **Henry**[5] **Christian Mayer** (*Mary*[4], *James*[3], *John*[2], *John*[1]), b. 3 March 1844 in New York, d. 21 May 1915 in Philadelphia, buried at Laurel Hill Cemetery.[345] He married first on 24 November 1869, **Nina Coppee Stevens**, born 23 December 1848 in Philadelphia.[346] He married second in Philadelphia on 16 May 1875, **Mary Fisher Lewis**,[347] born 13 June 1850 in Philadelphia, daughter of George T. and Sally (Fisher) Lewis.[348]

Child of Henry[5] C. and Nina (Stevens) Mayer:
  i. Christina[6] Stevens Mayer, b. 7 December 1871 in Newton, Massachusetts.[349]

Children of Henry[5] C. and Mary (Lewis) Mayer, all born in Pennsylvania.
  ii. George[6] Lewis Mayer, b. 7 August 1876.[350]
  iii. Ethel[6] M. Mayer, b. November 1878.[351]
  iv. Henry[6] C. Mayer, b. July 1883.[352]

29. **Mary**[5] **Abby Mayer** (*Mary*[4], *James*[3], *John*[2], *John*[1]), b. 14 September 1848 in Washington, D.C., d. 19 August 1915, in Ipswich, Massachusetts.[353] She married in Brookline, Massachusetts, on 3 June 1868, **John Singleton Copley Greene**.[354] He was born in Waltham, Massachusetts, on 13 October 1845, the son of Rev. J. S. Copley Greene,[355] d. 9 November 1872 in Berlin, Germany.[356]

Children of J.S. Copley and Mary[5] Abby (Mayer) Greene:
  i. Belle[6] Greene, b. 20 August 1870 in Brookline, Massachusetts.[357]
  ii. Henry[6] Copley Greene, b. 21 November 1871 in Vienna, Austria.[358]

30. **Richard**[5] **McCall McCulloh** (*William*[4], *James*[3], *John*[2], *John*[1]), b. February 1858 in Donaldsonville, d. 1 February 1911 in Donaldsonville.[359] He married in Donaldsonville on 17 February 1881, **Bertha M. Bercegeay**,[360] born October 1859 in Louisiana, daughter of Augustin Bercegeay.[361]

Children of Richard[5] McCall and Bertha (Bercegeay) McCulloh, both born in Donaldsonville:
   i.   Richard[6] McCulloh, b. 24 July 1883.[362]
   ii. William[6] J. McCulloh, b. April 1892.[363]

31. **Abby**[5] **Sears McCulloh** (*William*[4], *James*[3], *John*[2], *John*[1]), b. 27 February 1865 in Donaldsonville, d. 17 June 1936, in New Orleans.[364] She married in New Orleans on 21 April 1884, **Emile J. Delvaille**,[365] b. January 1862 in Louisiana,[366] d. 24 June 1908 in New Orleans.[367]

Children of Emile J. and Abby[5] (McCulloh) Delvaille, all born in New Orleans:
   i.   Anita[6] Delvaille, b. May 1885.[368]
   ii. Soline[6] Delvaille, b. February 1889.[369]

32. **Caroline**[5] **McCulloh** (*James*[4], *James*[3], *John*[2], *John*[1]), b. 16 February 1852 in New York City, d. 7 January 1936 in Birmingham, Alabama. She married in Englewood, New Jersey, in 1871, **William Lemmon**,[370] b. 22 October 1836 in Maryland, son of William P. and Susan Lemmon.[371]

Children of William and Caroline[5] (McCulloh) Lemmon, all born in Englewood:
   i.   Mary[6] Nelms Lemmon, b. October 1871,[372] d. 7 January 1934, Marietta, Georgia.[373]
   ii.   George[6] Nelms Lemmon, b. 11 November 1873,[374] d. 9 January 1960, Birmingham.[375]
   iii. Isabel[6] McCulloh Lemmon, b. 10 May 1876, d. 22 June 1936, Marietta.[376]
   iv.   William[6] Presstman Lemmon, b. 2 September 1878, d. 28 August 1955, Marietta.[377]
   v.   Clarita[6] M. Lemmon, b. April 1881.[378]
   vi.   Fanny[6] Lemmon, b. 10 September 1883, d. 23 March 1885.[379]
   vii. Robert[6] Stell Lemmon, b. 26 June 1885,[380] d. 3 March 1964, New Canaan, Conn.[381]

33. **Charles**[5] **Sears McCulloh** (*James*[4], *James*[3], *John*[2], *John*[1]), b. 1 July 1856 at Riverdale, New York, d. 26 December 1940 in Miami Beach, Florida.[382] He married first at St. George's Church in New York City, 23 April 1889, **Kate Monteath Mayo,**[383] b. 13 July 1858 in Yonkers, New York, daughter of Sylvanus and Marie Louise (Ritter) Mayo.[384] He married second in Richmond, Virginia, October 1926, **Jessie Olivia Burton,** born 1884.[385]

Child of Charles[5] S. and Kate (Mayo) McCulloh:
   i.   Katharine[6] Mayo McCulloh, b. 23 August 1893 in New York City,[386] d. 14 July 1979 in Olean, New York.[387]

34. **Allan McCulloh** (*James*[4], *James*[3], *John*[2], *John*[1]), b. 27 September 1858, Ossining, New York, d. 5 May 1932 in New York City.[388] He never married.

35. **Robert**[5] **Lee McCulloh** (*James*[4], *James*[3], *John*[2], *John*[1]), b. 31 August 1860 in New York, most likely Ossining, d. 20 December 1922 in Toronto, Canada.[389] He married first at the Englewood Presbyterian Church, 16 October 1883, **Hetty Louise Tilyon,**[390] born 18 December 1858 in Brooklyn, New York, daughter of Vincent and Emma Tilyon.[391] He married second in Toronto, Canada, 1 June 1899, **Eleanor Bell,**[392] born about 1867 in Toronto, daughter of Thomas and Emma (Somers) Bell.[393] No record of children was found for either marriage.

36. **Walter**[5] **McCulloh** (*James*[4], *James*[3], *John*[2], *John*[1]), b. 24 October 1862 in Ossining, New York, d. 1954 in Niagara Falls, New York, and is buried at Oakwood Cemetery.[394] He married in 1896, **Caroline Wright** who was born in Canada, 1856, daughter of George and Christina Wright.[395]

Adopted daughter of Walter[5] and Caroline (Wright) McCulloh:[396]
   i.   Dorothy[6] A. McCulloh, b. 16 May 1906 in England,[397] d. 30 September 1996 in Amherst, New York.[398]

37. **James**[5] **Sears McCulloh** (*James*[4], *James*[3], *John*[2], *John*[1]), b. 5 September 1868 in Englewood, d. 6 July 1957 in Rye, New York.[399] He married in

Philadelphia, 27 May 1898, **Sarah May (White) Gause,** b. 21 May 1866 in Philadelphia.[400] She had previously been married to Harlan Victor Gause, an author and writer, by which she had a daughter, Mildred.[401]

Children of James[5] S. and Sarah May (White) McCulloh:
  i.   Mildred[6] Gause McCulloh, b. 25 October 1888,[402] adopted after 1898, d. 8 October 1958.[403]
  ii. Gordon[6] McCulloh, b. 30 March 1899 in New York City.[404]

38. **Abby[5] Sears McCulloh** (*James[4], James[3], John[2], John[1]*), b. 8 March 1870 in Englewood, d. 20 May 1934 in Hindhead, Surrey, England.[405] She married in Englewood, 12 January 1896, **Arthur Lloyd Roberts.** They had no children.

39. **Russell[5] Sturgis Hubbard** (*Adelaide[4], James[3], John[2], John[1]*), b. 26 June 1863 in Westerly, NJ. He married **Elizabeth Perry.**[406]

Children of Russell[5] Sturgis and Elizabeth (Perry) Hubbard:
  i.   Russell[6] Sturgis Hubbard, Jr., b. 8 September 1902.[407]
  ii. John[6] P. Hubbard, b. 26 October 1903.[408]
  iii. James[6] DeWolf Hubbard, b. 7 December 1906.[409]

40. **Lucy[5] Sturgis Hubbard** (*Adelaide[4], James[3], John[2], John[1]*), b. 19 July 1872 in Massachusetts, d. 2 January 1927 in Philadelphia.[410] She married in Philadelphia in 1897, **William Hamilton Jefferys,**[411] b. 3 July 1871 in Philadelphia.[412]

Children of William H. and Lucy[5] S. (Hubbard) Jefferys:
  i.   Nancy[6] Jefferys, b. September 1897 in Philadelphia.[413]
  ii. Lucy[6] Jefferys, b. 18 March 1904 in China.[414]
  iii. Adelaide[6] McCulloh Jefferys, b. 23 March 1907 in China.[415]
  iv. William[6] H. Jefferys, Jr., b. 27 May 1916 in Philadelphia.[416]

41. **Sullivan**[5] **Warren Sturgis** (*Margaret*[4], *James*[3], *John*[2], *John*[1]), b. 24 April 1868 in Boston. He married in Lenox, Massachusetts, 26 July 1899, **Edith Stuart Barnes**.[417]

Children of Sullivan[5] W. and Edith (Barnes) Sturgis:
- i. Susan[6] B. Sturgis, b. 2 August 1900 in Manchester, Massachusetts.[418]
- ii. Edith[6] Sturgis, b. 16 April 1903 in Groton, Massachusetts.[419]
- iii. Somers[6] Hayes Sturgis, b. 14 October 1904 in Groton, Massachusetts.[420]
- iv. Warren[6] Sturgis, b. 26 November 1912 in Cambridge, Massachusetts.[421]

42. **Edward**[5] **Sturgis** (*Margaret*[4], *James*[3], *John*[2], *John*[1]), b. 24 April 1868 in Boston, d. 1939 in Milton, Massachusetts.[422] He married in Boston, 14 January 1902, **Josephine Putnam**.[423]

Children of Edward[5] and Josephine (Putnam) Sturgis:
- i. Edward[6] J. Sturgis, b. 25 July 1904 in Lucerne, Switzerland.[424]
- ii. George[6] Putnam Sturgis, b. 23 July 1905 in Lucerne, Switzerland.[425]
- iii. Howard[6] O. Sturgis, b. 9 September 1906 in Massachusetts.[426]
- iv. Harriet[6] Lowell Sturgis, b. 15 February 1908 in Andover, Massachusetts.[427]
- v. Josephine[6] Lowell Sturgis, b. 22 February 1910 in Andover.[428]
- vi. Charles[6] Russell Sturgis, b. 7 February 1913 in Andover.[429]

43. **James**[5] **McCulloh Sturgis** (*Margaret*[4], *James*[3], *John*[2], *John*[1]), b. 13 November 1872 in Boston, d. 18 October 1959, Belmont, Massachusetts, buried Forest Hills Cemetery.[430] He never married.

Notes

Chapter 1: "A Child of Sorrow"

1. All births and dates appear in Appendix. James W. McCulloh was born 5 February 1789.

2. James McCulloh to John McCulloh, 12 March 1789, 29 March 1789, 25 July 1789, Baltimore, MS 2110, reel 2 (1787-1794) frames 196, 201, 222, *John McCulloh Papers*, Maryland Historical Society, Baltimore, Maryland (hereafter cited as McCulloh MS 2110).

3. Ronald E. Shaffer, church historian, Old Pine Conservancy, personal letter to author, 2 May 2016; "Signatures to Duffield's call, 1771," Old Pine Conservancy.

4. "George Duffield, Revolutionary Patriot," *Journal of the Presbyterian Historical Society* (1943-1961) 33, no. 1 (1955): 4, 19, 21, http://www.jstor.org/stable/23325396; "The Old Pine Story," Old Pine Street Church, http://www.oldpine.org; Ronald E. Shaffer, personal letter to author, 2 May 2016.

5. "Muster Rolls Relating to the Associators and Militia, City of Philadelphia," John B. Linn and William H. Egle, editors, *Pennsylvania Archives Series*, 6th ser., vol. 1 (Harrisburg: Clarence M. Busch, 1895), 522, 523; "The history of Fort Mifflin," Fort Mifflin on the Delaware, http://www.fortmifflin.us/the-history/.

6. "The history of Fort Mifflin."

7. Keyser, *Memorials of Col. Jehu Eyre*, 421; "U.S. Revolutionary War Pension and Bounty-Land Warrant Application Files, 1800-1900," digital image 791, entry for Anna McCulloh, widow of John McCulloh, file no. W4489.

8. "U.S. Revolutionary War Pension and Bounty-Land Warrant Application Files, 1800-1900," digital images 754, 770, 771, http://www.ancestry.com, entry for Anna McCulloh, widow of John McCulloh, file no. W4489, cited from NARA M804, roll 1674; "Muster Rolls Relating to the Associators and Militia, City of Philadelphia," *Pennsylvania Archives Series*, 6th ser., vol. 1, 522, 523; Peter D. Keyser, "Memorials of Col. Jehu Eyre," *Pennsylvania Magazine of History and Biography*, Vol. 3 (1879), 418-420.

9. "U.S. Revolutionary War Pension and Bounty-Land Warrant Application Files, 1800-1900," digital images 754, 770, 771, entry for Anna McCulloh, widow of John McCulloh, file no. W4489; Keyser, *Memorials of Col. Jehu*

Eyre, 415-417; The *Pennsylvania Archives Series* was searched in regards to these battles.

10. "Muster Rolls Relating to the Associators and Militia, City of Philadelphia," *Pennsylvania Archives Series*, 6th ser., vol. 1, 538-540, 1st ser., vol. 7-2, 371.

11. "U.S. Revolutionary War Pension and Bounty-Land Warrant Application Files, 1800-1900," digital images 764, 819, 821, 823, 825; "A General Return of Militia Officers Belonging to the City of Philadelphia and District," *Pennsylvania Archives Series*, 6th ser., vol. 1, 551,553; "A List of the Field Officers commanding the City of Philadelphia and Districts Militia," *Pennsylvania Archives Series*, 6th ser., vol. 1, 565; "A General Return of Officers Duly Elected and Nominated Agreeable to the Militia Law of this State in the City of Philadelphia and Districts," *Pennsylvania Archives Series*, 6th ser., vol. 3, 1208.

12. Ronald E. Shaffer, personal letter to author, 2 May 2016; *Statutes at Large of Pennsylvania from 1662-1801*, Vol. 10, p. 317; Philadelphia, Pennsylvania, Deeds, D-16: 525, John McCulloh and Ann, his wife, to Ferguson McElwaine, Paul Cox, and William Henry, 7 September 1782, Old Pine Conservancy, Philadelphia.

13. Andrew Todd, Jr. affidavit, 24 July 1781, Margaret McCulloh affidavit, 19 May 1783, McCulloh MS 2110, reel 1 (1773-1786), frame 30, 54; "Finding aid," McCulloh MS 2110, p. 1; Charles Hardy III, *McCulloch family history*, (Self Published, 1998), 4, Oldfields School Archives, Sparks Glencoe, Maryland.

14. John McCulloh to Samey, 9 April 1796, Philadelphia, McCulloh MS 2110, reel 3 (1795-1800) frame 116, 117; Hardy, *McCulloch family history*, 6.

15. Andrew McCulloh to Isabella McCulloh, 9 October 1798, 18 October 1798, Germantown, McCulloh MS 2110, reel 3, frames 411-413; Andrew Todd to John McCulloh, 9 June 1799, Virginia, McCulloh MS 2110, reel 3, frames 482, 483.

Chapter 2: Life as Child

16. John McCulloh and Anna Bringhurst were married 8 April 1790.

17. Envelope to Maj. John McCulloh, 7 September 1782, Philadelphia, McCulloh MS 2110, reel 1, frame 40, McCulloh Family Papers, Maryland Historical Society, Baltimore, Maryland; Philadelphia, Pennsylvania, 1783 Assessment Book, Dock Ward, p. 37, John McCulloh, board

mercht, Records of the Office of Comptroller General, archive roll 366, "Pennsylvania, Tax and Exoneration, 1768-1801," http://www.ancestry.com; "Inventory of the personal estate of John McCulloh," 20 April 1800, McCulloh MS 2110, reel 3, frames 567-569.

18. Anna McCulloh, "Family Expenses Book," 1800-1801, MS 1770, Box 1, (1800-1827), McCulloh Family Collection, 1800-1853, Maryland Historical Society, Baltimore, Maryland.

19. "Bill from Francis Springer," 1794, McCulloh MS 2110, reel 3.

20. Charles Hardy III, *McCulloch family history*, 1998, 6, Oldfields School Archives, Sparks Glencoe, Maryland; "Mary McCulloh to Andrew McCulloh, 4 September 1802, Philadelphia," McCulloh MS 2110, reel 4 (1809-1834), frame 127.

21. "Nat Irish to Andrew McCulloh, 19 April 1800, Western Pennsylvania," McCulloh MS 2110, reel 3; McCulloh family papers (no date), Typed description and notes from *Journal of a Voyage in the ship Washington*, by Samuel McCulloh, 1796, passed down from a great granddaughter of James W. McCulloh, privately held by author, 2016.

22. "J. W. McCulloh to Samuel McCulloh, 22 December 1809, Philadelphia," McCulloh MS 2110, reel 5, frame 72.

23. "John McCulloh, will, written 28 October 1797, probated 23 April 1800," McCulloh MS 2110, reel 3, frames 572-574.

24. "Inventory of the personal estate of John McCulloh, 20 April 1800," McCulloh MS 2110, Reel 3; "Relative value of the U.S. dollar from 1744," Measuring Worth, *https://www.measuringworth.com/uscompare/*.

25. Samuel McCulloh to Andrew McCulloh, 16 May 1800, Philadelphia, McCulloh MS 2110, reel 3, frame 597.

26. Ibid, 21 May 1800, frame 600.

27. Anna McCulloh to Andrew McCulloh, 27 August 1801, Philadelphia, McCulloh MS 2110, reel 4 (1801-1808), frame 51; Anna McCulloh to Samuel McCulloh, letter 10 February 1810, Mary McCulloh, to Dear Brother, 11 October 1810, Philadelphia, McCulloh MS 2110, reel 5, frame 75, 97.

28. J. W. McCulloh to Samuel McCulloh, 13 April 1801, Philadelphia, McCulloh MS 2110, reel 4, frame 38, 39.

29. Anna McCulloh to Andrew McCulloh, 17 July 1801, Philadelphia, MS 2110, reel 4, frame 48.

30. Mary McCulloh to Andrew McCulloh, 8 January 1803, Margaret McCulloh to Samuel McCulloh, 9 June 1804, Philadelphia, McCulloh MS 2110, reel 4, frames 137, 233.

31. Andrew McCulloh to Anna McCulloh, no date, MS 2110, reel 6 (1835-1848), frame 195.

32. Dale Taylor, *The writer's guide to everyday life in Colonial America, from 1607-1783*, (Cincinnati, Ohio : Writer's Digest Books, 1997), 263; Aubrey C. Land, Lois Green Carr, Edward C. Papenfuse, *Law Society, and Politics in Early Maryland: proceedings of the first conference on Maryland History, June 14-15, 1974* (Baltimore, Johns Hopkins University Press : 1977), 217; Anna McCulloh to Andrew McCulloh, 10 February 1810, Philadelphia, McCulloh MS 2110, reel 5, frame 76.

33. "J. W. McCulloh to Andrew McCulloh, 22 December 1809, Philadelphia," McCulloh MS 2110, reel 5, frames 72, 73.

Chapter 3: Service in the War of 1812

34. Hardy, *McCulloch family history*, 8.

35. "Index to Compiled Service Records of Volunteer Soldiers who served during the War of 1812," James W. McCulloch, NARA M602, roll 137, http://www.fold3.com; Command Sergeant Major James Clifford, USA Ret., "Battles that Saved America: North Point and Baltimore 1814," https://armyhistory.org/battles-that-saved-america-north-point-and-baltimore-1814/.

36. William M. Marine, *The British Invasion of Maryland, 1812-1815*, (Baltimore, Md : Genealogical Publishing Co., Inc., 1977), 112.

37. Hardy, *McCulloch family history*, 8.

Chapter 4: A Family of Ten

38. Bayley Ellen Marks, *Hilton Heritage*, (Baltimore, Catonsville Community College Printing Services : 1993), 9; "Valuable farm for sale," *Baltimore Patriot*, 23 February 1828, p. 1, col. 6, http://www.genealogybank.com; 1820 U.S. Census, Baltimore County, Maryland, Baltimore District 1, p. 192, James W McCulloh, http://www.ancestry.com, citing NARA M33, roll 41.

39. *In Memoriam*, 6.

40. *In Memoriam*, 8, 13; Anna McCulloh to Andrew McCulloh, 13 June 1801, Philadelphia, McCulloh MS 2110, reel 4, frame 42.

41. *In Memoriam*, 12.

42. Hardy, *McCulloch family history*, 11; Margaret McCulloh to Samuel McCulloh, 24 January 1832, Philadelphia, McCulloh MS 2110, reel 5, frame 440, 441; "Princeton University General Catalogue of the College of New Jersey, 1746-1896," p. 80, Richard Sears McCulloh, U.S. School Catalogues, 1765-1935, *http://www.ancestry.com*; Milton Halsey Thomas, *Professor McCulloh of Princeton, Columbia and Points South*, (Princeton, N.J. : publisher not identified, 1947), 19.

43. Benjamin F. Shearer, ed, *Home front heroes: a biographical dictionary of Americans during wartime*, "McCulloh, Richard Sears (1818-1894)," 570.

44. "Catalogue of the officers and students of Jefferson College, 1843," p .6, William J. M'Culloh, U.S. School Catalogues, 1765-1935, *http://www.ancestry.com*; "Princeton University General Catalogue of the College of New Jersey, 1746-1896," p. 80.

45. "Catalogue of the officers and students of the University of Harvard, 1836," p. 19, Henry Christian Mayer, "U.S. School Catalogues, 1765-1935," *http://www.ancestry.com*; "Maryland Marriages, 1666-1970," database, Baltimore, Henry C. Mayer and Mary L. McCulloh (1842), *https://www.familysearch.org*; "For Rent to Lease," *Baltimore Sun*, 20 March 1844, p. 4, col. 1, *http://www.genealogybank.com*.

46. "Coroner's Inquest," *New York Commercial Advertiser*, 7 March 1846, p. 1, *http://www.genealogybank.com*; 1850 U.S. Census, Washington D.C., pop. sch., Washington Ward 1, p. 59B, dwelling 892, family 945, Mary Mayer, *http://www.ancestry.com*, citing NARA M432, roll 56.

47. *In Memoriam*, 15,16.

48. *In Memoriam*, 11, 17, 24, 28.

49. *In Memoriam*, 26-29.

50. 1855 Massachusetts State Census, Hampshire County, pop. sch., Northampton, dwelling 717, family 844, John P. Hubbard, Length of stay based on birth of children; 1860 U.S. Census, Washington County, Rhode Island, pop. sch., Westerly, p. 423, family 116, John P. Hubbard, citing NARA M653, roll 1211; 1880 U.S. Census, Jefferson County, West

Virginia, pop. sch., Potomac, ED 8, p. 149B, dwelling 151, family 152, John P. Hubbard, citing NARA T9, roll 1405, all from *http://www.ancestry.com*.

51. *In Memoriam*, 27-31.

52. *In Memoriam*, 51-53.

53. Hardy, *McCulloch family history*, 11, 16, 17.

54. "Death comes to Mr. James W. McCulloh at 7 O'clock," obituary, *The Daily Hot Blast* (Anniston, Alabama), 4 May 1897, p. 1; Charles R. Rode, compiler, *New York City Directory*, (New York, N.Y., 1852), 325, "U.S. City directories, 1822-1995," *http://www.ancestry.com*; New York City Landmarks Preservation Commission, *Riverdale Historic District*, (1990), 7, *http://www.nyc.gov/html/lpc*.

55. "History," Wave Hill, New York Public Garden and Cultural Center, *https://www.wavehill.org/about/history/*.

56. Hardy, *McCulloch family history*, 18, 19; Rode, *New York City Directory*, 1852, 82, *https://www.fold3.com*; "James McCulloh," obituary, *New York Tribune*, 6 May 1897, p. 7, *http://www.genealogybank.com*.

57. H. Wilson, compiler, *New York City Directory*, (New York, N.Y., John F. Trow, 1863), 546, also subsequent years by the same title: (1864) 542, (1866) 609, (1868) 647, (1870) 694, (1874) 811, (1875) 1813, *https://www.fold3.com*; "Death comes to Mr. James W. McCulloh at 7 O'clock."

58. "Confederate Papers Relating to the Citizens or Businesss firms, 1861-1865," document 33, Richard S. McCulloh, digital image 24, *http://www.fold3.com*, citing NARA M346, roll 623.

59. R. S. McCulloh, "Report of the Secretary of the Treasury of scientific investigations in relation to sugar and hydrometers," (Washington: Wendell and Van Benthuysen, 1848), *https://catalog.loc.gov*.

60. "From the Newark Daily of Thursday," *New York Spectator*, 29 October 1849, p. 1; "The Inauguration of Richard S. McCulloh," *Centinel of Freedom* (Newark, New Jersey), 5 December 1854, p. 2, both from *http://www.genealogybank.com*.

61. 1860 U.S. Census, Essex County, New Jersey, pop. sch., Orange Ward 3, p. 375, dwelling 668, family 858, Annie L. Brown, *http://www.ancestry.com*, citing NARA M653, roll 690.

62. 1850 U.S. Census, Ascension County, Louisiana, pop. sch., p. 39, dwelling 313, family 314, J Wm McCullogh, *http://www.ancestry.com*, accessed 29

Feb. 2016, citing NARA M432, roll 299; "Appointments by the President," *Daily Union* (Washington, D.C.), 17 March 1854, p. 2, col. 5; "Five Hundred Dollars Reward," *New Orleans Times –Picayune*, 27 March 1858, p. 5, col. 1, both from http://www.genealogybank.com; 1860 U.S. Census, Ascension County, Louisiana, slave sch., Donaldsonville, p. 86, W J McCulloh, http://www.ancestry.com.

63. 1830 U.S. Census, Baltimore County, Maryland, Baltimore District 1, p. 39 Samuel McCullok, http://www.ancestry.com, citing NARA M19, roll 55; "Know all men by these present," 13 August 1839, Baltimore, McCulloh MS 2110, reel 6, frame 126; Baltimore County, Maryland, Wills, Vol. 23, image 13, will of Samuel McCulloh, 1849, http://www.familysearch.org.

Chapter 5: Heading in a Different Direction

64. Sarah J. Purcell, *The early national period*, (New York : Facts on File, 2004), 230, 237; Alfred Cookman Bryan, *History of State Banking in Maryland*, (Balitmore : John Hopkins Press, 1899), 35, 67; "Death of James W. McCulloh," obituary, *Baltimore Sun*, 27 June 1861, p. 1, col. 3, http://www.genealogybank.com.

65. "McCulloh accounts, bills, receipts," MS 1356, folder 1817-1818, McCulloh Family Papers, Maryland Historical Society, Baltimore, Maryland.

66. David S. Bogen, "The scandal of Smith and Buchanan: the skeletons in the McCulloh vs. Maryland closet," Maryland Law Forum, vol. 9, no. 4, June 1985, 128-131, Maryland State Archives Special Collections; Sarah McCulloh to Samuel McCulloh, 17 Dec. 1817, Philadelphia, McCulloh MS 2110, reel 5, frame 226.

67. Bogen, *Scandal of Smith and Buchanan*, 129; *McCulloch v. Maryland*, 17 U.S. (4 Wheat.) 316 (1819).

68. "Background Summary & Questions," *McCulloch v. Maryland* (1819), Landmark Cases of the U.S. Supreme Court, http://landmarkcases.org/en/Page/364/Background_Summary__Questions_; Daniel A. Farber, *The story of McCulloh: Banking on National Power* (2003), 691, 692, Berkeley Law Scholarship Repository, http://scholarship.law.berkeley.edu/cgi/viewcontent.cgi?article=1446&context=facpubs; "John White, Esq. has been appointed Cashier," *New York Commercial Advertiser*, 22 May 1819, p. 2, http://www.genealogybank.com; Land, *Law, Society, and Politics*, 219.

69. Bogen, "Scandal of Smith and Buchanan," 130, 131; Marks, *Hilton Heritage*, 9.

70. "Baltimore, April 12," *Alexandria Gazette* (Virginia), 17 April 1823, p. 2, col. 2, http://www.genealogybank.com; Bogen, "Scandal of Smith and Buchanan," 131.

71. See appendix for sources.

72. Margaret McCulloh to Samuel McCulloh, 20 December 1825, Philadelphia, McCulloh MS 2110, reel 5, frame 333.

73. "Historical list, Speakers of the House of Delegates," Archives of Maryland online, http://msa.maryland.gov/msa/speccol/sc2600/sc2685/html/hsespkrs.html; Hardy, *McCulloch family history*, 9; James D. Dilts, *The Great Road: the building of the Baltimore & Ohio, the nation's first railroad 1828-1855*, (Stanford, Calif. : Stanford University Press, 1993), 46, 106; National Park Service, *Chesapeake and Ohio Canal: Race to the West*.

74. "Testimony taken before the Joint Committee of the Senate and House of Delegates of Maryland," p. 51, digital image, http://www.ancestry.com; Peter Kumpa, "In the aftermath of the 1835 riots: a victory for the wealthy," 15 October 1990, digital image, *Baltimore Sun*, http://articles.baltimoresun.com/1990-10-15/news/1990288143_1_general-smith-fellow-citizens-samuel-smith.

75. "A schedule of the value of the lands," McCulloh MS 2110, reel 6, frames 273-282; Wm Johnston to Samuel McCulloh, 26 March 1833, McCulloh MS 2110, reel 5, frame 456; John Claypoole to Samuel McCulloh, 24 May 1836; Samuel McCulloh to Wm McCloud, 2 August 1836; John Gilpin to Samuel McCulloh, 28 Oct. 1837, McCulloh MS 2110, reel 6, frames 67, 70, 94.

76. Sarah B. McCulloh to James W. McCulloh, 29 August 1834, McCulloh MS 2110, reel 5, frame 498; *William McCulloh vs Samuel McCulloh*, no date; William McCulloh to James W. McCulloh, 15 September 1836, McCulloh MS 2110, reel 6, frames 70, 72.

77. "We the subcribers," 26 June 1838, McCulloh MS 2110, reel 6, frame 113; Ann McCulloh to James W. McCulloh, 26 June 1838, , McCulloh MS 2110, reel 6, frame 114.

78. James W. McCulloh to Samuel McCulloh, 2 February 1841, McCulloh MS 2110, reel 6, frames 157, 158; Bound papers, MS 1770, box 3, McCulloh Family Collection, 1800-1853.

79. "Whig Festival in Baltimore," *Alexandria Gazette* (Virginia), November 16, 1835, p. 3, col. 1; "Franklin Turnpike Road," *Baltimore Gazette and Daily Advertiser*, January 18, 1828, p. 3, col. 2; "Canton Company of Baltimore," *New York Commercial Advertiser*, June 12, 1837, p. 2, col. 4; "Cross Cut Canal," *Alexandria Gazette* (Virginia), March 1, 1839, p. 3, col. 4, all from http://www.genealogybank.com; *Matchetts's Baltimore Directory for 1837* (Baltimore, Maryland), 15, Archives of Maryland online, http://aomol.msa.maryland.gov; "For the Promotion of Science and Literature," *Wilmingtonian and Delaware Advertiser* (Wilmington, Delaware), May 10, 1827, http://www.ancestry.com; "Address of the Trustees of the University of Maryland," 1830, U.S. College Student Lists, 1763-1924, http://www.ancestry.com.

80. "We regret to learn," *Alexandria Gazette* (Virginia), 20 September 1839, p. 2, col. 4, http://www.genealogybank.com.

81. "James W. McCulloh, Esq.," *Baltimore Sun*, 30 March 1842, p. 2, col. 2; "The office of First Comptroller of the Treasury," *Daily National Intelligencer* (Washington, D.C.), 2 April 1842, p. 3, col. 4; "General Agency at Washington," *Daily Union* (Washington, D.C.), 30 June 1847, p. 2, col 6, all from http://www.genealogybank.com; Robert Mayo, *The Treasury Department and its various fiscal bureaus, their origin, organization, and practical operations, illustrated: being supplement to synopsis of Treasury instructions for administration of revenue laws affecting commercial and revenue system of U. S.* (Washington : printed by Wm Q. Force, 1847), 59-61, https://books.google.com.

Chapter 6: A Tragic End

82. Hardy, *McCulloch family history*, 10, 19; 1855 New York State Census, New York County, pop. sch., New York City, Ward 3, ED. 2, sheet 34, dwelling 106, family 184, James W. McCulloh, http://www.ancestry.com; 1860 U.S. Census, Essex County, New Jersey, pop. sch., Orange, Ward 3, p. 375, dwelling 668, family 858, Annie L. Brown, citing NARA M653, roll 690; 1870 U.S. Census, Norfolk County, Massachusetts, pop. sch., Brookline, p. 140, dwelling 779, family 1020, Anna Brown, citing NARA M653, roll 634, both at http://www.ancestry.com.

83. Hardy, *McCulloch family history*, 22.

84. Hardy, *McCulloch family history*, 19; *In Memoriam*, 59; 1860 U.S. Census, Middlesex County, Massachusetts, pop. sch., Newton, p. 803, dwelling

25619, family 2853, John S C Greene, *http://www.ancestry.com*, citing NARA M653, roll 510.

85. 1860 U.S. Census, Middlesex Co., Mass., pop. sch., Newton, p. 803, dwelling 2561, family 2853, Mary Mayer; 1870 U.S. Census, Norfolk, Massachusetts, pop. sch., Brookline, p. 132B, Mana Upham, *http://www.ancestry.com*, citing NARA M593, roll 634.

86. *In Memoriam*, 59; 1870 U.S. Census, Essex County, Massachusetts, pop. sch., Manchester, p. 759A, dwelling 233, family 338, Margaret Sturgis, citing NARA M593, roll 611; McPherson, *Oldfields School: a feeling of family*, p. 14; 1920 U.S. Census, Suffolk County, Massachusetts, pop. sch., Boston Ward 8, ED 231, p. 10B, dwelling 106, family 126, Margaret Sturgis, , citing NARA T625, roll 742, both at *http://www.ancestry.com*.

87. Hardy, *McCulloch family history*, 16.

88. Bound papers, 11 July, 1849, MS 1770, Box 3 (1835-1840); "Maryland probate estate and guardianship files, 1796-1940", Allegany County, Vol. M, James W. McCulloh, 31 August 1887, digital images 6-15, *http://familysearch.org*.

Chapter 7: The Civil War and Beyond

89. "From the Newark Daily of Thursday," *New York Spectator*, 29 October 1849, p. 1; "The Inauguration of Richard S. McCulloh," *Newark Centinel of Freedom* (New Jersey), 5 December 1854, p. 2, both from *http://www.genealogybank.com*; 1855 New York State Census, New York County, New York, ED. 2, p. 34, dwelling 106, family 184, Richard S. McCulloh, *http://www.ancestry.com*.

90. Singer, Jane, *The Confederate Dirty War: Arson, Bombings, Assassination, and Plots for Chemical and Germ Attacks on the Union* (Jefferson, N.C.: McFarland & Co., 2005), 100.

91. Milton Halsey Thomas, Professor McCulloh of Princeton, Columbia and Points South, (Princeton, N.J.: publisher not identified, 1947), 25.

92. "Confederate Papers Relating to the Citizens or Businesss firms, 1861-1865," document 33, Richard S. McCulloh, digital image 6, *http://www.fold3.com*, citing NARA M346, roll 623.

93. "Confederate Papers," Richard S. McCulloh, digital image 27-30.

94. Singer, *The Confederate Dirty War*, 102-112.

95. Singer, *The Confederate Dirty War*, 114, 116; 1870 U.S. Census, Rockbridge County, Virginia, pop. sch., Lexington, p. 485B, dwelling 336, family 336, R S McCulloh, http://www.ancestry.com, citing NARA M593, roll 1675; Richard Sears McCulloh, "Treatise on the mechanical theory of heat and its applications to the steam-engine." http://www.worldcat.org.

96. "Prof. Richard S. McCulloh," *Ouachita Telegraph* (Monroe, Louisiana), 23 November 1877, p. 1, col. 4, https://www.newspapers.com.

97. Mary King McPherson, *Oldfields School, 1867-1989: a feeling of family* (Glencoe, Md, Oldfields School: 1989), x, xvi.

98. McPherson, *Oldfields School*, 1, 2.

99. McPherson, *Oldfields School*, 3, 10.

100. McPherson, *Oldfields School*, 17; "John S. McCulloch," obituary, *Baltimore Sun*, 6 July 1900, p. 7, col. 5, http://www.genealogybank.com.

101. Hardy, *McCulloch family history*, 23.

102. "Wm J. McCulloh," obituary," *New Orleans Times*, 17 August 1877, p. 3, col. 1, http://www.genealogybank.com; "4th Regiment, Louisiana Infantry," brief history, https://familysearch.org; Louisiana Regiments Index, http://laahgp.genealogyvillage.com, p. 2.

103. Edwards' Annual Directory… in the City of New Orleans, (New Orleans, Southern Pub. Co., 1870), p. 390, "U.S. City directories, 1822-1995," http://www.ancestry.com; 1880 U.S. Census, Orleans County, Louisiana, pop. sch., New Orleans Ward 7, ED 52, p. 617D, Abby McCoulloh, http://www.ancestry.com, citing NARA T9, roll 462.

104. "Wm J. McCulloh," *New Orleans Times*, 17 August 1877.

105. Adaline W. Sterling, *The Book of Englewood* (Englewood, N.J. : The Mayor and Council of the City of Englewood, 1922), p. 48, 56, http://archive.org; *At the Century Mark, First Presbyterian Church, Englewood, New Jersey*, 4, http://www.ancestry.com; 1860 U.S. Census, Bergen County, New Jersey, pop. sch., Hackensack Township, p. 76, dwelling 507, family 535, James McCulloch; http://www.ancestry.com, citing NARA M653, roll 683.

106. Sterling, *The Book of Englewood*, p. 104, 105, 110.

107. "The Water Getters," *New York Truth*, 1 August 1883, p. 3, col. 3, http://www.genealogybank.com; "Forcing out the secretary," *New York Times*, 8 July 1886, p. 8, col. 2, http://www.ancestry.com; "James W. McCulloh," *Harpers Weekly*, August 1886.

108. "Death comes to Mr. James W. McCulloh," *The Daily Hot Blast* (Anniston, Alabama), 4 May 1897.

109. Ibid.

110. *In Memoriam*, 69, 85-91, 96.

111. "William I. Brown," obituary, *Baltimore Sun*, 5 January 1900, p. 7, col. 6; "Annie L. Brown," obituary, *Baltimore Sun*, 9 March 1911, p. 6, col. 5, both at http://www.genealogybank.com; 1910 U.S. Census, Baltimore County, Maryland, pop. sch., Baltimore, Ward 11, ED 160, p. 5B, dwelling 97, family 98, Annie L. Brown, http://www.ancestry.com, citing NARA T624, roll 556.

112. 1910 U.S. Census, Philadelphia County, Pennsylvania, pop. sch., Philadelphia Ward 22, ED 430, p. 4A, dwelling 55, family 56, Adelaide Hubbard, http://www.ancestry.com, citing NARA T62, roll 1396; "Mother follows daughter in death," *Philadelphia Inquirer*, 15 October 1917, p. 10, col. 6, http://www.genealogybank.com.

113. "Mary L. Upham," obituary, *Boston Herald*, 17 December 1, 1916, p. 3, col. 4; http://www.genealogybank.com; "U.S. Passport Applications, 1795-1925," Mary L. Upham, (1876), digital image 914, NARA roll 212, 1 Feb. 1876 – 30 April 1876; digital image 396, NARA roll 368, 23 April 1891-30 April 1891; digital image 524, NARA roll 422, 24 May 1894 – 31 May 1894; digital image 264, NARA roll 495, 1 Sept. 1897 – 30 Sept. 1897, all at http://www.ancestry.com.

Chapter 8: Grandchildren, a Lasting Legacy

114. "Catalogue of the officers and students of Columbia College, 1865-1866," p.15, U.S. School Catalogues, 1765-1935, http://www.ancestry.com; 1875 New York State Census, Richmond County, Castleton, ED 1, sheet 65, dwelling 384, family 511, George S. McCullough; H. Wilson, compiler, *New York City Directory*, (New York, New York, John F. Trow, 1889), 1246, "U.S. City directories, 1822-1995," http://www.ancestry.com.

115. "Catalogue of the officers and students of Columbia College, 1870-71," p.15; McPherson, *Oldfields School*, 8; "Death of Prof. R. D. Irving," *Wisconsin State Journal*, June 1, 1888, p. 8, col. 2, http://www.genealogybank.com; "Roland D. Irving," Dane, Wisconsin probate records, Box 104, digital image 904, "Wisconsin Wills and probate Records, 1800-1987," http://www.ancestry.com; 1900 U.S. Census, Baltimore County, Maryland, population schedule, Baltimore City, Election Dist. 10, p. 9B, dwelling 172, family 173, Abby L

Irving, http://www.ancestry.com, accessed 20 March 2016, citing NARA T623, roll 607.

116. 1900 U.S. Census, Baltimore County, Maryland, pop sch., Baltimore City, ED 10, p. 9B, dwelling 172, family 173, Abby L Irving, http://www.ancestry.com, citing NARA T623, roll 607; McPherson, *Oldfields School,* 17.

117. "U.S. Passport Applications, 1795-1925," Duncan McCulloh (1886), digital image 238, NARA roll 282, 1 May 1886 – 31 May 1886; McPherson, *Oldfields School,* 31.

118. 1900 U.S. Census, Baltimore County, Maryland, Baltimore City, ED 10, p. 9B, dwelling 173, family 174, Rev. Doncan McCulloh; McPherson, *Oldfields School,* 25; 1920 U.S. Census, Baltimore County, Maryland, pop. sch., Baltimore City, ED 10, p. 9A, dwelling 178, family 181, Duncan McCulloh, *http://www.ancestry.com,* citing NARA T625, roll 655.

119. "U.S. Passport Applications, 1795-1925," Duncan McCulloch (1924), digital image 224, NARA M1490, certificate no. 383489.

120. J.H. Baldwin, compiler, *Baldwin's Directory of the Oranges,* (Orange, New Jersey, 1900), 160, James W. McCulloch "U.S. City directories, 1822-1995," http://www.ancestry.com; Anson Phelps Stokes, *Stokes Records: notes regarding the ancestry and lives of Anson Phelps Stokes and Helen Louisa (Phelps) Stokes* (New York: Privately printed, 1915), 3:47, 65, 155, 159, www.archive.org; "U.S. Passport Applications, 1795-1925," James William McCulloch, (1923), digital image 652, NARA roll 212, 1 Feb. 1876 – 30 April 1876.

121. Manifest, *Majestic,* 18 September 1923, p. 58, James McCulloch, "New York Passenger Lists, 1820-1957," microfilm T715, roll 3374, 1897-1957; Manifest, *Berengarian,* 7 October 1927, p. 52, James McCulloch, microfilm T715, roll 4145, 1897-1957, both at "New York Passenger Lists, 1820-1957," *http://www.ancestry.com.*

122. 1900 U.S. Census, Alleghany County, Pennsylvania, pop. sch., Oakmont borough, ED 466, p. 6A, dwelling 108, family 109, John A McCullough, citing NARA T623, roll 1370; 1910 U.S. Census, Grafton County, New Hampshire, pop. sch., Hanover, ED 87, p. 14A, dwelling 28, family 32, Mary D McCullah, citing NARA T624, roll 861; 1910 U.S. Census, Allegheny, Pennsylvania, pop. sch., McKeesport, Ward 6, ED 129, p. 19B, dwelling 249, family 377, John A McCulloch, citing NARA T624, roll 1295; 1930 U.S. Census, Denver, Colorado, pop. sch., Denver, ED 114, p. 6B, dwelling 3, family 3, John A McCulloch, citing NARA T626, roll 237, all at *http://www.ancestry.com.*

123. Brantz Mayer, *Memoir and Genealogy of the Maryland and Pennsylvania family of Mayer: which originated in the free Imperial City of Ulm Wurtemburg, 1495-1878* (Baltimore: privately printed, 1878), 54, https://www.familysearch.org.

124. "U.S. Passport Applications, 1795-1925," Henry C. Mayer, (1872), digital image 1288, NARA roll 183, 9 May 1872 – 22 May 1872; "Missionary dies," Henry C. Mayer obituary, *Harrisburg Patriot*, (Pennsylvania) 22 May 1915, p. 1, col. 8, http://www.genealogybank.com.

125. 1850 U.S. Census, Washington D.C., pop. sch., Washington, Ward 1, p. 59B, dwelling 892, family 945, Mary Mayer, http://www.ancestry.com, citing NARA M432, roll 56; 1860 U.S. Census, Middlesex County, Massachusetts, pop. sch., Newton, p. 803, dwelling 2561, family 2853, Mary Mayer, citing NARA M653, roll 510, both at http://www.ancestry.com; "Massachusetts Marriages, 1841-1915," database, John Singleton Copley Greene and Mary Abby Mayer (1868), https://www.familysearch.org.

126. Secretary's Report, Harvard Class of 1867, p. 38; "U.S. Passport Applications, 1795-1925," Dr. J. S. C. Greene, Jr., (1871), digital image 305, NARA roll 171, 1 March 1871 – 18 April 1871; "Dr. J. S. Copley Greene," death notice, *Boston Daily Advertiser*, 14 November 1872, p. 4, col. 3, http://www.genealogybank.com.

127. Isaac Costa, compiler, *Gopsill's Philadelphia City Directory*, (Philadelphia, Pennsylvania, James Gopsill, 1874), 564, also subsequent year (1875), 617, "U.S. City directories, 1822-1995," http://www.ancestry.com; 1910 U.S. Census, Suffolk County, Massachusetts, pop. sch., Boston, Ward 11, ED 1424, p. 8B, dwelling 91, family 113, Mary A. Greene, http://www.ancestry.com, citing NARA T624, roll 618; "U.S. Passport Applications, 1795-1925," Mary A. Greene., Belle Greene, Henry Copley Greene (1897), digital images 264, 267, 286, NARA roll 422, 27 May 1897 – 31 May 1897.

128. "Senator McCulloh dead," obituary, *New Orleans Times-Picayune*, 2 February 1911, p. 9; "Bachelors of Laws," *New Orleans Times-Picayune*, 9 May 1880, p. 11, col. 2; "Weaving the web around Jules Valentine," *New Orleans Times-Picayune*, 18 September 1904, p. 12, col. 2, all at http://www.genealogybank.com; "Membership in the Louisiana State Senate, 1880-Present," compiled by Arthur E. McEnany, 2012.

129. "Senator McCulloh dead," *New Orleans Times-Picayune*, 2 February 1911, p. 9.

130. Ibid.

131. 1880 U.S. Census, Orleans County, Louisiana, pop. sch., New Orleans, Ward 7, ED 52, p. 617D, Abby McCoulloh, citing NARA T9, roll 462; 1900 U.S. Census, Orleans County, Louisiana, pop. sch., New Orleans, Ward 6, ED 56, p. 2B, dwelling 25, family 38, Emile Delvaille, citing NARA T623, roll 572; 1910 U.S. Census, Orleans County, Louisiana, pop. sch., New Orleans, Ward 7, ED 108, p. 5B, dwelling 103, family 112, Abby Delvaille, citing NARA T624, roll 521; 1930 U.S. Census, Orleans County, Louisiana, pop. sch., New Orleans, Ward 7, ED 117, p. 20A, dwelling 289, family 314, Emile Delvaille, citing NARA T626, roll 805, all at *http://www.ancestry.com*; *Soard's New Orleans City Directory, 1933* (New Orleans, 1933), p. 426, "U.S. City directories, 1822-1995," *http://www.ancestry.com*.

132. 1880 U.S. Census, Bergen County, New Jersey, pop. sch., Englewood, ED 2, p. 244A, Caroline Lemmon, citing NARA T9, roll 77; 1900 U.S. Census, Bergen County, New Jersey, pop. sch., Englewood, Ward 4, ED 13, p. 11A, dwelling 201, family 222, Caroline Lemmons, citing NARA T623, roll 954; 1920 U.S. Census, New York County, New York, pop. sch., Manhattan, Assembly District 13, ED 977, p. 16A, family 977, Corilin Lemmon, citing NARA T625, roll 1209; 1930 U.S. Census, Cobb County, Georgia, pop. sch., Militia District 898, ED 15, p. 5B, dwelling 122, family 138, Caroline Lemon citing NARA T625, roll 1209; all at *http://www.ancestry.com*.

133. "Charles S. McCulloh," obituary, *New York Times*, 27 December 1940, author's clippings.

134. 1900 U.S. Census, New York County, New York, pop. sch., Manhattan, ED 462, p. 18A, dwelling 33, family 457, Charles McCulloh, citing NARA T623, roll 1103; 1910 U.S. Census, New York County, New York, pop. sch., Manhattan, Ward 12, ED 525, p. 11A, dwelling 38, family 274, Chas S McCulloh citing NARA T624, roll 1021; 1920 U.S. Census, New York County, New York, pop. sch., Manhattan Assembly District 21, ED 1435, p. 4B, dwelling 17, family 69, Charles McCulloh, citing NARA T625, roll 1224; 1930 U.S. Census, New York County, New York, pop. sch., Manhattan, ED 541, p. 3B, dwelling 122, family 138, Charles S McCulloh, citing NARA T626, roll 1566, all at *http://www.ancestry.com*.

135. "Cherry Diamond Yacht Club," *New York Herald*, 16 February, 1892, p. 8, *http://www.genealogybank.com*; Scott Family papers in author's possession.

136. "Wheelmen out for M'Kinley," *New York Tribune*, 31 October 1896, p. 10, col. 3, *http://www.genealogybank.com*.

137. Interview with grandson, Grant Scott, Jr., in 1990; "Charles S. McCulloh," *New York Times*, 27 December 1940.

138. "Catalogue of the officers and students of Columbia College, 1877," p. 130, digital image 157, U.S. School Catalogues, 1765-1935, *http://www.ancestry. com*; 1910 U.S. Census, New York County, New York, pop. sch., Manhattan, Ward 22, ED 1387, p. 5B, dwelling 51, family 89, Allan McCulloh, citing NARA T624, roll 1048; 1930 U.S. Census, New York County, New York, pop. sch., Manhattan, ED 552, p. 22A, dwelling 109, family 336, Allan McCulloh, citing NARA T636, roll 1566, both at *http://www.ancestry.com*.

139. "New York Passenger Lists, 1820-1957," database, Allan McCulloh, *http:// www.ancestry.com*, citing NARA T715, 1889, 1897, 1899, 1912, 1921, 1924-26, 1928, 1930-31; "Deaths," Allan McCulloh, *New York Times*, 7 May 1932, *http://www.ancestry.com*.

140. "Ontario, Canada Marriages, 1801-1928," , Robert Lee McCulloh and Eleanor Bell, (1899) *http://www.ancestry.com*, Archives of Ontario, Series MS932, roll 97, York County, p. 81; 1910 U.S. Census, Westmoreland County, Pennsylvania, pop. sch., Greensburg, Ward 2, ED 128, p. 1B, dwelling 11, family 16, Robert L McCulloh, *http://www.ancestry.com*, citing NARA T624, roll 1429; "Ontario, Canada Deaths, 1869-1938," Robert Lee McCulloh, (1922), *http://www.ancestry.com*, Archives of Ontario, Series MS935, roll 286, York County, deaths, p. 436.

141. "Across the Niagara Gorge," *Watertown Daily Times* (New York), 15 February 1896, p. 9, col. 3, *http://www.genealogybank.com*; "Conference of New York Mayors," *Watertown Daily Times*, 22 May 1911, p. 2, col. 4, *http://www.genealogybank.com*; 1910 U.S. Census, Albany County, New York, pop sch, Albany, Ward 14, ED 68, p. 3B, dwelling 62, family 91, Walter McCulloh, citing NARA T624, roll 921; 1920 U.S. Census, Niagara County, New York, pop. sch., Niagara Falls, Ward 2, ED 100, p. 6B, dwelling 85, family 125, Walter McCulloh, citing NARA T625, roll 1241; 1940 U.S. Census, Niagara County, New York, pop. sch., Niagara Falls, ED 32, p. 2A, dwelling 319, family 260, Walter McCulloh, citing NARA T627, roll 2696; all at *http://www.ancestry.com*; 1925 New York State Census, Niagara County, pop. sch., Niagara Falls, AD 02, ED 01, p. 13, Walter McCulloh, *http://www.ancestry.com*; *Niagara Falls City Directory, 1959* (Buffalo, NY, R. L. Polk, 1959), 646, "U.S. City directories, 1822-1995," *http://www.ancestry. com*.

142. "James McCulloh of Bell System," obituary, *New York Times*, 5 July 1957, author's private collection.

143. "Milestones in AT&T History," History of AT&T, http://www.corp.att.com/history/milestones.html.

144. "James McCulloh of Bell System," *New York Times*; John William Leonard, *History of the City of New York, 1609-1909: From the Earliest Discoveries to the Hudson-Fulton celebration; together with brief biographies of men representative of the business interests in the city*," (New York: Journal of commerce and commercial bulletin, 1910), 466.

145. "James McCulloh dies," *New York Herald Tribune*, 6 July 1957.

146. Ibid.

147. 1910 U.S. Census, Westchester County, New York, pop. sch., Rye, ED 124, p. 12B, dwelling 204, family 220, James S McCullogh, http://www.ancestry.com, citing NARA T624, roll, 1092; 1905 New York State Census, Westchester County, pop. sch., Rye, AD 02, ED 03, p. 5, James McCulloh; 1915 New York State Census, Westchester County, pop. sched., Rye, AD 04, ED 05, p. 14, James S McCulloh, both at http://www.ancestry.com.

148. Manifest, Kensington, July 1894, p. 12, Abby S. McCulloch; Manifest, *Compania*, 19 February 1896, p. 6, Arthur L. Roberts, both at "UK, Incoming Passenger Lists," 1878-1960, http://www.ancestry.com; Manifest, *Umbria*, 2 Sept 1893, p. 11, Arthur L. Roberts; Manifest, *Aurania*, 5 September 1894, p. 11, Arthur L. Roberts; Manifest, *Etruria*, 11 May 1896, p. 21, Arthur L. Roberts; Manifest, *Britannic*, 14 August 1896, p. 12, Arthur L. Roberts, all at "New York Passenger Lists, 1820-1957," http://www.ancestry.com; "New Jersey, Marriages, 1670-1980," Englewood, Arthur L. Roberts and Abby S. McCulloh, https://:www.familysearch.org; "James W. McCulloh," *Anniston Blast* (Alabama), 4 May 1897.

149. 1901 census of Wales, Denbighshire, Abergele, Dist. 4, p. 5, Abby Sears Roberts, http://www.ancestry.com, citing RG13, Piece 5237, Folio 16; Manifest, *Lucania*, 24 October 1903, Abbey S. Roberts, Manifest, *Mauretania*, 18 January 1908, Abbey Sears Roberts, Manifest, *Mauretania*, 28 January 1911, Abbey S. Roberts, all at "New York Passenger Lists, 1820-1957," http://www.ancestry.com; 1911 census of England, Cheshire, Heswall, Arthur Lloyd Roberts, "England and Wales Census, 1911," database, https://familysearch.org.

150. "U.S. Passport Applications, 1795-1925," Russel S. Hubbard (1890), digital image 63, NARA roll 355, 24 June 1890 – 30 June 1890; *Gospill's Philadelphia City Directory, 1894* (Philadelphia, James Gospill's Sons, 1894), 955; William H. Boyd, compiler, *Boyd's Business Directory Philadelphia,* (Philadelphia, William H. Boyd, 1904), 407, both at "U.S. City directories, 1822-1995," http://www.ancestry.com.

151. 1910 U.S. Census, Philadelphia County, Pennsylvania, pop. sch., Philadelphia Ward 27, ED 667, p. 4A, dwelling 49, family 50, Lucie Jefferys, http://www.ancestry.com, citing NARA T623, roll 1469; Manifest, *Chiyo Maru*, 21 December 1911, Dr. William H. Jefferys, "Hawaii, Honolulu Passenger Lists, 1900-1953," http://www.ancestry.com, citing NARA microfilm A3422, roll 32, 1911-1912; 1911 census of England, London, England, Dist. 1, Paddington, W. Hamilton Jefferys, http://www.ancestry.com, citing RG14, Piece 75; 1920 U.S. Census, Philadelphia County, New York, pop. sch., Philadelphia, Ward 22, ED 629, p. 6B, dwelling 86, family 87, William H. Jefferys, http://www.ancestry.com, citing NARA T625, roll 1624.

152. Grace Williamson Edes, *Annals of the Harvard Class of 1852*, (Cambridge, Ma.: Privately Published, 1922), 452, digital image, http://www.ancestry.com; "U.S. Passport Applications, 1795-1925," Sullivan Warren Sturgis (1890), digital image 206, NARA roll 44, Vol. 82; 1900 U.S. Census, Middlesex County, Massachusetts, pop. sch., Groton, ED 762, p. 14A, dwelling 369, family 336, Sullivan Sturgis, citing NARA T623, roll 659; 1920 U.S. Census, Suffolk County, Massachusetts, pop. sch., Boston, Ward 8, ED 236, p. 11B, dwelling 158, family 176, Sturgis W Sturgis, citing NARA T625, roll 742, both at http://www.ancestry.com.

153. Manifest, *President Polk*, 25 November 1922, p. 26, S. Warren Sturgis, "U.K. Incoming Passenger Lists, 1878-1960," http://www.ancestry.com, citing microfilm Class BT6, piece 722; Manifest, *Maurentania*, 28 July 1923, p. 16, S. Warren Sturgis, "New York Passenger Lists, 1820-1957," http://www.ancestry.com, citing microfilm T715, roll 4145, 1897-1957.

154. "U.S. Passport Applications, 1795-1925," Edward Sturgis (1890), digital image 205 and Sullivan Warren Sturgis (1890), digital image 206; Manifest, *Devonian*, 4 November 1902, p. 64, Rev. Edward Sturgis, "Massachusetts Passenger and Crew Lists, 1820-1963," http://www.ancestry.com, citing microfilm T843; "U.S. Passport Applications, 1795-1925," Edward Sturgis, (1904), digital image 121, citing NARA roll 55, Vol. 109, Switzerland.

155. 1910 U.S. Census, Essex County, Massachusetts, pop. sch., Andover, ED 264, p. 8B, dwelling 128, family 138, Edward Sturgis, citing NARA T624, roll 580; 1920 U.S. Census, Norfolk County, Massachusetts, pop. sch., Milton, ED 207, p. 18B, dwelling 393, family 404, Edward Sturgis, citing NARA T625, roll 722; 1930 U.S. Census, Norfolk County, Massachusetts, pop. sch., Milton, ED 66, p. 10A, dwelling 196, family 214, Edward Sturgis, citing NARA T626, roll 935, all at http://www.ancestry.com.

156. Frederick S. Mead, ed., *Harvard's Military Record in the World War*, (Boston: Harvard Alumni Assoc., 1921), 1080, http://www.ancestry.com; 1920 U.S. Census, Suffolk County, Massachusetts, pop. sch., Boston, Ward 8, ED 1387, p. 10B, dwelling 106, family 126, James McCulloh Sturgis, http://www.ancestry.com, citing NARA T625, roll 742.

Chapter 9: The British Connection

157. Hardy, *McCulloch family history*, 5; "UK, American Loyalist Claims, 1776-1835," George Roupell, *National Archives of the UK*, American Loyalist claims, class AO13, Series 11, Piece 135, claims G, image 63, 64, http://www.ancestry.com; City of London, St. Dunstan in the West, marriages, George Boone Roupell and Frances Browne McCulloh (1794), image 1, "London, England, Church of England Marriages and Banns, 1754-1921," http://www.ancestry.com.

158. "England Marriages, 1538-1973," transcription, Saint George the Martyr Queen Square, Durham, Samuel McCulloh and Eleanor McCulloh (1824), http://www.findmypast.com.

159. Samuel McCulloh to sister, 8 March 1840, McCulloh MS 2110, reel 6, frame 135.

160. "U.S. Passport Applications, 1795-1925," Mary L. Upham, (1876), digital image 914, NARA roll 212, 1 Feb. 1876 – 30 April 1876; digital image 396, NARA roll 368, 23 April 1891-30 April 1891; digital image 524, NARA roll 422, 24 May 1894 – 31 May 1894; digital image 264, NARA roll 495, 1 Sept. 1897 – 30 Sept. 1897, all at http://www.ancestry.com; "New Jersey, Marriages, 1670-1980," Englewood, Arthur L. Roberts and Abby S. McCulloh, https://www.familysearch.org; "New York Passenger Lists, 1820-1957," database, Allan McCulloh, http://www.ancestry.com, citing NARA T715, 1889, 1897, 1899, 1912, 1921, 1924-26, 1928, 1930-31.

Appendix: McCulloh Family Lineage

161. McCulloh family papers (no date), privately held by author, 2016.

162. McCulloh MS 2110, reel 2, frame 21, 111, 366.

163. Ibid.

164. "Scotland Births and Baptisms, 1564-1950," database, Barr by Girvan, Ayrshire, Scotland, Robert McCulloh, https://www.familysearch.org, FHL 1041333.

165. Ibid, William McCulloh.

166. Ibid, William McCulloh.

167. Ibid, John McCulloh.

168. Ibid, James McCulloh.

169. "Scotland Births and Baptisms, 1564-1950," database, Dailly, Ayrshire, Scotland, Sarah McCulloh, https://www.familysearch.org, FHL 1041337.

170. Ibid, Anne McCulloh.

171. McCulloh family papers (no date), privately held by author, 2016.

172. Ibid.

173. "North West Kent Burials Transcriptions," Charlton, Robert McCulloch (1789), North West Kent History Society, https://www.findmypast.com.

174. McCulloh family papers (no date), privately held by author, 2016.

175. George Boone Roupell to John McCulloh, 20 April 1798, London, McCulloh MS 2110, reel 3, frame 338.

176. Monument for Francis Browne Roupell (1770-1853), memorial #154261243, http://www.findagrave.com; 1851 England Census, Middlesex, Marylebone, Dist. 2b, p. 45, household 617, Frances B. Roupell, http://www.ancestry.com, citing Class H0107, Piece 1487, Folio 106.

177. Ibid; Francis McCulloh, will, Sussex, England, McCulloh MS 2110, reel 5, frame 179.

178. Ibid; Francis McCulloh, will, Sussex, England, McCulloh MS 2110, reel 5, frame 179.

179. Third Presbyterian Church Tombstones, Plot 22 – 70, Capt. Wm McCulloh, Old Pine Conservancy, Philadelphia, Pennsylvania; Philadelphia County, Pennsylvania, City of Philadelphia, Will abstract, Vol. S, 259,

William McCulloh, 1783, *http://usgwarchives.net/pa/philadelphia/willsabst.htm.*

180. Philadelphia, Old St. Paul's Church, marriages, William McCullough and Hanna Williams, (1773), image 18, "Pennsylvania and New Jersey Church and Town Records, 1708,1985," *http://www.ancestry.com.*

181. "Maryland Register of Wills, 1629-1999," Baltimore, Vol. 4, image 15, Margaret McCulloh (1784), *http://www.familysearch.org.*

182. John McCulloh Family Bible (no date), "U.S. Revolutionary War Pension and Bounty-Land Warrant Application Files, 1800-1900," digital images 745-748, 752, *http://www.ancestry.com,* accessed 21 March 2016, entry for Anna McCulloh, widow of John McCulloh, file no. W4489, cited from NARA M804, roll 1674.

183. John McCulloh Family Bible; Third Presbyterian Church Tombstones, Plot 22 – 73, Major John McCulloh, Old Pine Conservancy, Philadelphia, Pennsylvania.

184. John McCulloh Family Bible.

185. Westmoreland County, Pennsylvania, Wills, Vol. 14 (1905-1908), 360, will of Andrew Todd, 1791, *http://www.ancestry.com.*

186. John McCulloh Family Bible.

187. John McCulloh Family Bible.

188. Josiah Greenville Leach, *History of the Bringhurst Family with notes on the Clarkson, De Peyster and Boude Families,* (Philadelphia: J. P. Lippincott, 1901) 34, 35.

189. "Mrs. Anna McCulloh," death notice, *Philadelphia Inquirer,* 30 May 1848, p. 2, *http://www.genealogybank.com.*

190. John McCulloh Family Bible.

191. Silas Dinsmore to Samuel McCulloh, 7 August 1809, New Orleans, McCulloh MS 2110, reel 5, frame 52.

192. John McCulloh Family Bible.

193. McCulloh family papers (no date), privately held by author, 2016.

194. John McCulloh Family Bible.

195. "Sarah B. McCulloh," death notice, *New York Tribune,* 28 May 1867, p. 5, *http://www.genealogybank.com*

196. John McCulloh Family Bible.

197. "Ann Smith McCulloh," death notice, *Philadelphia Inquirer*, 17 August 1853, p. 2, http://www.genealogybank.com.

198. Hardy, *McCulloch family history*, 4; "Maryland Register of Wills, 1629-1999," Baltimore County, Vol. 6, p. 72, image 37, Samuel Mcculloh (1798), http://www.familysearch.org.

199. James McCulloh to John McCulloh, 6 Sept. 1783, Prince Ann, Maryland, McCulloh MS 2110, reel 1, frame 74.

200. "Maryland Register of Wills, 1629-1999," Baltimore County, Vol. 6, p. 72, image 37, Samuel McCulloh (1798).

201. "Maryland Church Records, 1668-1995," database, Baltimore, Edward Pannell, father, Sarah, mother, https://www.familysearch.org, FHL 13699; "Maryland Wills and Probate Records, 1604-1998," Baltimore, Vol. 15, p. 279, image 157, Edward Pannell (1835), http://www.familysearch.org.

202. Hardy, *McCulloch family history*, 4.

203. Philadelphia, Old St. Paul's Church, marriages, David Williamson and Anne McCullough, (1773), image 19.

204. "Maryland Church Records, 1668-1995," database, Baltimore, Levi Pierce and Mary Elizabeth Williamson, https://www.familysearch.org, FHL 13699.

205. "Maryland Marriages, 1655-1850," database, Baltimore, Humphrey Pierce and Ann Williamson, http://www.ancestry.com.

206. "Samuel McCulloh," obituary, *Washington Daily Union* (District of Columbia), 31 December 1848, p. 3, col. 5, http://www.genealogybank.com.

207. Boston Marriage Publications, 1798-1807, vol. 7, Samuel McCulloh and Isabella Williamson (1803), "Massachusetts, Town and Vital Records, 1620-1988," http://www.ancestry.com.

208. "England Marriages, 1538-1973," transcription, Durham, Samuel McCulloh and Eleanor McCulloh (1824)," http://www.ancestry.com.

209. "Maryland Register of Wills, 1629-1999," Baltimore, Vol. 23, image 13, Samuel McCulloh (1849), http://www.familysearch.org.

210. "Maryland Marriages, 1655-1850," database, Baltimore, Jacob Green and Ann Eliza McCulloh, http://www.ancestry.com.

211. Ashbel Green, *The life of Ashbel Green, V. D. M.* (New York: Robert Carter & Bros., 1849), 405; digital images, *https://archive.org/details/lifeofashbelgreen00gree*; Finding Aid, Ashbel Green papers, Princeton University Library, *http://findingaids.princeton.edu/collections/C0257*.

212. Green, *The life of Ashbel Green, V. D. M*, 385.

213. Gravestone for Margaret Cummins (1852), memorial #132825984, *http://www.findagrave.com*.

214. Joseph M. Wilson, *The Presbyterian historical almanac and annual remembrance of the church*, (Philadelphia, Pa.: Joseph M. Wilson, 1859) vol. 6, 108.

215. Third Presbyterian Church Baptisms by hand of Rev. George Duffield, James Wm Benoi Todd, son of John and Ann McCullough, Old Pine Conservancy, Philadelphia, Pennsylvania.

216. "Death of James W. McCulloh," obituary.

217. "Maryland Marriages, 1666-1970," index, Baltimore, James W. McCulloh and Abby H. Sears, *https://www.familysearch.org*.

218. McCulloh family papers (no date), privately held by author, 2016.

219. "Abby S. McCulloh," obituary, *New York Tribune*, 24 December 1864, p. 5, *http://www.genealogybank.com*, accessed 26 February 2016.

220. McCulloh family papers (no date), privately held by author, 2016.

221. Third Presbyterian Church Baptisms, John Sears, son of John and Ann McCullough.

222. Gravestone for Richard Sears McCulloch (1818-1894), memorial #61676771, *http://www.findagrave.com*.

223. "U.S. Passport Applications, 1795-1925," Mary L. Upham, (1876), digital image 914, *http://www.ancestry.com*, citing NARA roll 212, 1 Feb. 1876 – 30 April 1876.

224. *In Memoriam*, 5.

225. McCulloh family papers, privately held by author, 2016.

226. Gravestone for Annie L. Brown (1829-1911), memorial #61609065, *http://www.findagrave.com*.

227. 1900 U.S. Census, Philadelphia County, Pennsylvania, pop. sch., Philadelphia, Ward 22, ED 490, p. 3A, dwelling 39, family 39, Ada Huttard, *http://www.ancestry.com*, citing NARA T623, roll 607.

228. Margaret Sturgis death record, "Massachusetts, Town and Vital Records, 1620-1988," http://www.ancestry.com.

229. Gravestone for Isabella Williamson McCulloch Green (1793-1865), memorial #95907067, http://www.findagrave.com.

230. Samuel S. Greene, *Genealogical sketch of the descendants of Thomas Green of Malden, Mass.* (Boston: Henry W. Dutton & Son, 1858), 56, digital image 295, http://www.ancestry.com.

231. "U.S. Passport Applications, 1795-1925," Ashbel Green, (1890), digital image 240, http://www.ancestry.com, citing NARA Emergency Passport Applications, 1877-1907, roll 44, vol. 82: England.

232. Gravestone for Anna Green Mactier (1827-1917), memorial #90137313, http://www.findagrave.com.

233. Gravestone for Dr. James S. Green (1829-1892), memorial #134848591, http://www.findagrave.com.

234. Gravestone for Robert Stockton Green (1831-1895), memorial #3882, http://www.findagrave.com.

235. Gravestone for Isabella Green (1834-1906), memorial #95907681, http://www.findagrave.com.

236. "Maryland Wills and Probate Records, 1604-1998," Baltimore, William S. McCulloh, (1850), http://www.ancestry.com.

237. Anne H. Wharton, *Genealogy of the Wharton Family of Philadelphia, 1664-1880* (Philadelphia: Collins, 1880), 53; Baltimore County, Maryland, Wills, Vol. 23, p. 1, will of Samuel McCulloh, (1849), image 15, "Maryland Register of Wills, 1629-1999," http://www.familysearch.org.

238. Baltimore County, Maryland, Wills, Vol. 23, p. 1, will of Samuel McCulloh, (1849).

239. Gravestone for John Sears McCulloch (1816-1900), memorial #61677927, http://www.findagrave.com.

240. "Maryland Marriages, 1666-1970," index, Baltimore, John S. McCulloh and Anna Austen.

241. Truman Abbe and Hubert Abbe Howson, *Robert Colgate the immigrant: a genealogy of the New York Colgates and some associated lines,* (New Haven, Ct.: Tuttle, Morehouse & Taylor Co., 1941), 80.

242. Gravestone for Anna Austen McCulloch (1824-1904), memorial #61677927, http://www.findagrave.com; "The Late Mrs. A. A. McCulloh," obituary, *Baltimore Sun*, 30 March 1904, p. 6, http://www.genealogybank.com, accessed 12 March 2016.

243. "New York, New York City Municipal Deaths, 1795-1949," George S. McCulloh (1925), http://www.familysearch.org, FHL 2168611.

244. Truman and Howson, *Robert Colgate the immigrant*, 175; 1900 U.S. Census, Baltimore County, Maryland, pop. sch., Baltimore City, Election Dist. 10, ED 44, p. 9B, dwelling 172, family 173, Abby L. Irving; http://www.ancestry.com, citing NARA T623, roll 607.

245. Gravestone for Anna Green McCulloch (1849-1928), memorial #61678341, http://www.findagrave.com.

246. Truman and Howson, *Robert Colgate the immigrant*, 175; Gravestone for Caroline A. McCulloch (1851-1898), memorial #61678341, http://www.findagrave.com; "Caroline Austen McCulloh," obituary, *New York Herald*, 6 November 1898, p. 1, col. 6; http://www.genealogybank.com.

247. "U.S. Passport Applications, 1795-1925," Duncan McCulloch, (1924), digital image 224, https://www.familysearch.org, citing NARA M1490, 2 January 1906 – 31 March 1925.

248. Ibid, Edward A. McCulloch (1887), digital image 740, citing NARA roll 288, 1 Feb. 1887- 28 Feb. 1887.

249. 1930 U.S. Census, Carroll County, Maryland, pop. sch., Freedom, ED 9, p. 7B, Edward A. McCullough, http://www.ancestry.com, citing NARA T626, roll 872.

250. "U.S. Passport Applications, 1795-1925," James William McCulloch, (1923), digital image, 652, citing NARA roll 2321, 29 June 1923 – 30 June 1923.

251. Truman and Howson, *Robert Colgate the immigrant*, 177.

252. Ibid.

253. Gravestone for John Austen McCulloch (1864-1938), memorial #61678684, http://www.findagrave.com; 1900 U.S. Census, Allegheny County, Pennsylvania, pop. sch., Oakmont borough, ED 466, p. 6A, dwelling 108, family 109, John A. McCullough; http://www.ancestry.com, citing NARA T623, roll 1370.

254. Gravestone for Richard Sears McCulloch (1818-1894), memorial #616767, http://www.findagrave.com.

255. "Married," *Alexandria Gazette* (Virginia), 9 January 1846, p. 3, col. 2, Richard S. McCulloh and Mary Stewart Vowell, http://www.genealogybank.com.

256. Gravestone for Margaretta Grace McCulloch (1847-1921), memorial #616767, http://www.findagrave.com.

257. "Mary L. Upham," obituary, *Boston Herald*, 1 December 1916, p. 3, col. 4, http://www.genealogybank.com.

258. "Maryland Marriages, 1666-1970," index, Baltimore, Henry C. Mayer and Mary L. McCulloh.

259. "Henry C. Mayer," obituary, *Daily Union* (Washington, D.C.), 7 March 1846, p. 3, col. 7, http://www.genealogybank.com.

260. "Massachusetts, Town and Vital Records, 1620-1988," Newton, p. 15, Henry Upham and Mary Louisa McCulloh, http://www.ancestry.com.

261. "Massachusetts Death Records, 1841-1915," database, Brookline, Henry Upham, http://www.ancestry.com.

262. "Maryland, Births and Christenings, index, 1662-1911," Susan Theresa Mayer, http://www.ancestry.com.

263. "U.S. Newspaper extractions from the Northeast, 1794-1930," *New York Evening Post*, Deaths 1856-1857, p. 95, Susan T. Mayer, http://www.ancestry.com.

264. Henry C. Mayer death certificate (1915), "Philadelphia, Pennsylvania, Death Certificates Index, 1803-1915," http://www.ancestry.com.

265. Brantz Mayer, *Memoir and Genealogy of the Maryland and Pennsylvania family of Mayer: which originated in the free Imperial City of Wurtembuerg, 1495-1878* (Baltimore: privately printed, 1878), 54, http://www.familysearch.org.

266. "U.S. Passport Applications, 1795-1925," Mary A. Greene, (1894), digital image 524, http://www.ancestry.com, citing NARA roll 422, 24 May 1894 – 31 May 1894.

267. New York, New York City Municipal Deaths, 1795-1949," Isabella Williamson McCulloh Greene (1870), FHL 1324545.

268. 1860 U.S. Census, Middlesex Co., Mass., pop. sch., Newton, p. 803, dwelling 2561, family 2853, Isabella W Greene.

269. "Rev. John Singleton Copley Greene," obituary, *Springfield Republican* (Massachusetts), 9 July 1872, p. 4, col. 3, http://www.genealogybank.com.

270. "U.S. Passport Applications, 1795-1925," Mary Amory Greene, (1891), digital image 287, citing NARA roll 368, 23 April 1891 – 30 April 1891.

271. "Massachusetts Births and Christenings, 1639-1915," database, Newton Corner, Margaret Greene, https://www.familysearch.org, FHL 1420998.

272. "W. J. McCulloh," death notice, *New Orleans Times-Picayune*, 20 August 1877, p. 8, col. 2; http://www.genealogybank.com.

273. "Louisiana Marriages, 1718-1925," database, William J. McCulloh and Adeline E. Bercegeay (1856), http://www.ancestry.com.

274. 1850 U.S. Census, Ascension County, Louisiana, pop. sch., p. 24A, dwelling 445, family 445, Adeline Bercegeay, http://www.ancestry.com, citing NARA M432, roll 229.

275. 1860 U.S. Census, Ascension County, Louisiana, pop. sch., Donaldsonville, p. 73, dwelling 539, family 539, James McCulloh, citing NARA M653, roll 407.

276. 1900 U.S. Census, Asension County, Louisiana, pop. sch., Donaldsonville Ward 3, ED 4, p. 11B, dwelling 223, family 239, Richard M McCulloh, http://www.ancestry.com, citing NARA T623, roll 557.

277. 1860 U.S. Census, Ascension Co., Louisiana, pop. sch., Donalsonville, p. 73, dwelling 539, family 539, W. J. McCulloh.

278. Gravestone for Abby S. McCulloch Delvaille (1865-1936), memorial #149814091, http://www.findagrave.com.

279. "Margie McCulloh," death notice, *New Orleans Times-Picayune*, 17 April 1870, p. 4, col. 3, http://www.genealogybank.com.

280. "James W. McCulloh," obituary.

281. McCulloh family papers (no date), privately held by author, 2016; Calhoun County, Alabama, Anniston, Wills, Vol. A, 150, will of James W. McCulloh, 1898, http://www.ancestry.com.

282. McCulloh family papers (no date), privately held by author.

283. "Alabama Deaths, 1908 -1974," database, Birmingham, Carolyn Lemmon, https://www.familysearch.org.

284. McCulloh family Bible (no date), inscription inside says, "Archy McCulloh from Mother, 1909", Henry Mayer McCulloh, privately held by author, 2016.

285. 1860 U.S. Census, Bergen County, Louisiana, pop. sch., Hackensack Twp., p. 76, dwelling 507, family 535, James McCulloch, https://www.fold3.com, citing NARA M653, roll 683.

286. McCulloh family Bible (no date), Charles Sears McCulloh, privately held by author, 2016.

287. "U.S. Passport Applications, 1795-1925," Allan McCulloh, (1921), digital image 675, citing NARA roll 1707, 3 August 1921 – 4 August 1921.

288. Gravestone for Robert Lee McCulloh (1860-1922), memorial #126243737, http://www.findagrave.com.

289. "U.S. Passport Applications, 1795-1925," Walter McCulloh, (1924), digital image 752, citing NARA roll 2642, 24 September 1924 – 26 September 1924.

290. "New York, New York City Municipal Deaths, 1795-1949," Archy McCulloh (1932).

291. "U.S. Passport Applications, 1795-1925," Mary Eaton McCulloh, (1896), digital image 219, citing NARA roll 479, 1 December 1896 – 31 December 1896.

292. "New York, New York City Municipal Deaths, 1795-1949," Mary McCulloh (1934).

293. "U.S. Social Security Applications and Claims Index, 1936-2007," James Sears McCulloh (1939), http://www.ancestry.com.

294. McCulloh family Bible (no date), Abby Sears McCulloh, privately held by author, 2016.

295. Ibid.

296. "New Jersey, Deaths and Burials, Index, 1798-1971," database, Englewood, Louis McCulloh (1877), http://www.ancestry.com.

297. "Annie L. Brown," obituary, *Baltimore Sun*, 9 March 1911, p. 6, col. 5, http://www.genealogybank.com.

298. "District of Columbia Marriages, 1811-1950," database, William J. Browne and Annie L. McCulloh, (1853) https://www.familysearch.org.

299. Gravestone for William I. Brown (1825-1900), memorial #616709377, http://www.findagrave.com.

300. Gravestone for W. McCulloh Brown (1854-1936), memorial #616709377, http://www.findagrave.com.

301. Ibid., Susan Theresa Brown (1862-1944).

302. McCulloh family papers privately held by author, 2016.

303. Kirk & Nice Funeral Home (Germantown, Philadelphia, Pennsylvania), for Adalaide Sears Hubbard, buried 14 October 1917, http://www.ancestry.com.

304. "Washington, DC, Marriages, 1826-50, database, John P. Hubbard and Adelaide S. McCulloh, http://www.ancestry.com, accessed 6 March 2016.

305. "Massachusetts, Birth Records, 1840-1915," Worthington, 1852, Jane Hubbard, http://www.ancestry.com; Kirk & Nice Funeral Home, Jane Hubbard, buried 27 February 1904.

306. John P. Hubbard birth record, "Massachusetts, Birth Records, 1840-1915," Northampton, 1853, John P. Hubbard.

307. 1855 Massachusetts State Census, Hampshire County, pop. sch., Northampton, reel 13, vol. 18, dwelling 717, family 844, Margaret Hubbard, http://www.ancestry.com.

308. "U.S. Newspaper extractions from the Northeast, 1794-1930", *New York Evening Post*, Deaths 1857-1858, p. 22, Margaret Hubbard.

309. James N. Arnold, *Vital Records of Rhode Island, 1636-1850*, Vol. 11, Church Records: 69, John Parkinson Hubbard, http://www.ancestry.com.

310. Ibid, Russel Sturgis Hubbard.

311. Ann McCulloh Hubbard death certificate (1927), "Philadelphia, Pennsylvania, Death Certificates, 1906-1963," http://www.ancestry.com; 1870 U.S. Census, Washington County, Rhode Island, pop. sch., Westerly, p. 399B, Anna W. Hubbard; http://www.ancestry.com, citing NARA T9, roll 597.

312. Arnold, *Vital Records of Rhode Island, 1636-1850*, 69, William Hubbard.

313. 1870 U.S. Census, Washington Co., Rhode Island, Waverly, p. 399B, John P. Hubbard.

314. Lucy S. Jefferys death certificate (1927), "Pennsylvania, Death Certificates Index, 1906-1963."

315. Edith Hubbard death certificate (1923), "Philadelphia, Pennsylvania, Death Certificates, 1906-1963."

316. "Massachusetts Births, 1841-1915," database, Boston, Sullivan Warren Sturgis (1868), http:www.familysearch.org.

317. "U.S. Passport Applications, 1795-1925," James McCulloh Sturgis, (1917), digital image 148, citing NARA roll 405, 18 Sept. 1917 – 20 Sept. 1917.

318. "Massachusetts Births, 1841-1915," database, Boston, Lucy C. Sturgis (1876).

319. "New York, New York City Municipal Deaths, 1795-1949," George S. McCulloh (1925), FHL 2168661.

320. "U.S. Newspaper extractions from the Northeast, 1794-1930", *New York Evening Post*, Marriages 1866-1870, p. 77, George Sears McCulloh and Elizabeth Irving, http://www.ancestry.com.

321. Truman and Howson, *Robert Colgate the immigrant*, 175.

322. "United States World War I Registration Cards, 1917-1918," District of Columbia, Robert Austen McCulloh, https://www.familysearch.org.

323. Truman and Howson, *Robert Colgate the immigrant*, 175.

324. "Maryland Marriages, 1666-1970," index, Baltimore, Abby McCulloh and Roland Irving.

325. "Death of Prof. R. D. Irving," obituary, *Wisconsin State Journal* (Madison), 1 June 1888, p. 8, col. 2, http://www.genealogybank.com.

326. "U.S. Newspaper extractions from the Northeast, 1794-1930", *New York Evening Post*, deaths, 1888, p. 44, Roland Duer Irving, http://www.ancestry.com.

327. New York, New York City Municipal Deaths, 1795-1949," Peter Irving (1944), FHL 2132191.

328. Truman and Howson, *Robert Colgate the immigrant*, 176.

329. "U.S. Passport Applications, 1795-1925," Duncan McCulloch, (1924), digital image 224, https://www.familysearch.org, citing NARA M1490, 2 January 1906 – 31 March 1925; "U.S. Newspaper extractions from the Northeast, 1794-1930," *New York Evening Post*, Marriages 1884-1890, p. 69, Rev. Duncan McCulloch and Mary Sterrett Carroll, http://www.ancestry.com.

330. "Vermont, St. Albans, Canada Border Crossings, 1895-1954," Mary Duncan McCulloh, (1924), https://www.familysearch.org, citing NARA M1461, roll 257, M240, Kenneth – M242, Peter O.

331. Gravestone for Duncan McCulloch (1898-1963), memorial #61449088, http://www.findagrave.com.

332. "North Carolina Deaths, 1931-1994," database, Chapel Hill, Ann Austin McCullock Hill, https://www.familysearch.org.

333. James W. McCulloch (1857-1938), memorial #158011039, http://www.findagrave.com.

334. St. Stephen's Episcopal Church Marriages, James Wm McCulloch and Jane Leavenwoth, p. 287, "Pennsylvania and New Jersey Church and Town Records, 1708-1985," http://www.ancestry.com.

335. "New York, New York Death Index, 1862-1948," Kings Co., Jane McCulloch (1887), http://www.ancestry.com.

336. "U.S. Passport Applications, 1795-1925," James William McCulloch, (1923), digital image 652, http://www.ancestry.com, citing NARA roll 2321, 29 June 1923 – 30 June 1923; Truman and Howson, *Robert Colgate the immigrant*, 177.

337. St. Stephen's Episcopal Church Baptisms, Paul Leavenworth McCulloch, p. 140, "Pennsylvania and New Jersey Church and Town Records, 1708-1985," http://www.ancestry.com.

338. "New Jersey Births and Christenings, 1660-1980," database, Orange, McCulloh, https://www.familysearch.org, FHL 589079.

339. Ibid, Elizabeth D. McCullack.

340. Manifest, *Majestic*, 18 September 1923, p. 58, Warren McCulloch, "New York Passenger Lists, 1820-1957," http://www.ancestry.com, citing microfilm T715, roll 3374, 1897-1957.

341. Ibid, Margaret McCulloch.

342. Gravestone for John Austen McCulloch (1864-1938), memorial #61678684, http://www.findagrave.com; 1930 U.S. Census, Denver County, Colorado, pop. sch., Denver, ED 114, p. 6B, dwelling 3, family 3, John A. McCulloh, http://www.ancestry.com, citing NARA T626, roll 237.

343. "U.S. Quaker Meeting Records, 1681-1935," Baltimore Monthly Members 1882-1906, Mary D. Shoemaker, p. 64-65, http://www.ancestry.com; 1900

U.S. Census, Allegheny County, Penn., Oakmont borough, ED 466, p. 6A, dwell. 108, fam.109, John A. McCullough.

344. Gravestone for Mary Dawson McCulloch (1865-1926), memorial #113514708, http://www.findagrave.com.

345. Henry C. Mayer death certificate (1915), "Philadelphia, Pennsylvania, Death Certificates Index, 1803-1915."

346. Mayer, *Memoir and Genealogy of the Maryland and Pennsylvania family of Mayer*, 54.

347. Holy Trinity Episcopal Church Marriages, Philadelphia, p. 196, Henry Christian Mayer and Mary Fisher Lewis, "Pennsylvania and New Jersey Church and Town Records, 1708-1985," http://www.ancestry.com.

348. Anne H. Wharton, *The Genealogy of the Wharton Family of Philadelphia, 1664-1880*, (Philadelphia, 1880), 54.

349. "Massachusetts Births, 1841-1915," database, Newton, Christina Stevens Mayer, (1871).

350. Mayer, *Memoir and Genealogy of the Maryland and Pennsylvania family of Mayer*, 54.

351. 1900 U.S. Census, Philadelphia County, Pennsylvania, Philadelphia, Ward 27, ED 653, p. 6B, dwelling 119, family 130, Ethel M. Mayer, http://www.ancestry.com, citing NARA T623, roll 1469.

352. Ibid, Henry C. Mayer.

353. "Massachusetts Deaths, 1841-1915," database, Ipswich, Mary A. Green, https://www.familysearch.org, FHL 240704.

354. "Massachusetts Marriages, 1841-1915," database, Brookline, John Singleton Copley Greene and Mary Abby Mayer, https://www.familysearch.org, FHL 1433026.

355. "U.S. Passport Applications, 1795-1925," Dr. J. S. C. Greene, Jr. (1871), digital image 305, citing NARA roll 171, 1 March 1871 – 18 April 1871.

356. "Dr. J. S. Copley Greene," death notice, *Boston Daily Advertiser*, 14 November 1872, p. 4, col. 3, http://www.genealogybank.com.

357. "U.S. Passport Applications, 1795-1925," Belle Greene (1894), digital image 267, citing NARA roll 495, 1 Sept. 1897 – 30 Sept. 1897.

358. Ibid, Henry Copley Greene, digital image 529, citing NARA roll 669, 1 Feb. 1905 – 28 Feb. 1905.

359. "Senator McCulloh Dead," obituary, *New Orleans Times-* Picayune, 2 February 1911, p. 9, http://www.genealogybank.com.

360. "Louisiana Marriages, 1718-1925," R. M. McCulloh and Bertha M. Bercegeay.

361. 1900 U.S. Census, Ascension County, Louisiana, Donaldsonville, Ward 3, ED 4, p. 11B, dwelling 223, family 239, Berth McCulloh; 1880 U.S. Census, Ascension County, Louisiana, pop. sch., Donaldsonville, Ward 3, ED 94, p. 80D, Berthe Bercegeay, http://www.ancestry.com, citing NARA T9, roll 447.

362. "U. S., World War I Draft Cards, 1917-1918," Massachusetts, Lynn City, Richard McCall McCulloh, http://www.ancestry.com.

363. "U.S. Social Security Death Index, 1935-2014," William McCulloh (1980), http://www.ancestry.com.

364. Gravestone for Abby S. McCulloh Delvaille (1865-1936), memorial #149814091, http://www.findagrave.com.

365. "New Orleans, Louisiana, Death Records Index, 1804-1949," Abby Sears McCulloh, (1936), http://www.ancestry.com.

366. 1900 U.S. Census, Orleans County, Louisiana, New Orleans Ward 6, ED 56, p. 2B, dwelling 25, family 38, Emile Devaille, http://www.ancestry.com, citing NARA T623, roll 572.

367. Gravestone for Emile J. Delvaille (1908), memorial #149814085, http://www.findagrave.com.

368. 1900 U.S. Census, Orleans Co., Louisiana, New Orleans Ward 6, ED 56, p. 2B, dwelling 25, family 38, Anita Delvaille.

369. Ibid, Soline Delvaille.

370. 1900 U.S. Census, Bergen County, New Jersey, pop. sch., Englewood, Ward 4, ED 13, p. 11A, dwelling 201, family 222, Wm Lemmons, http://www.ancestry.com, citing NARA T623, roll 954; William Presstman Lemmon death certificate (1955), "North Carolina, Death Certificates Index, 1909-1976," http://www.ancestry.com.

371. "Georgia Deaths, index, 1914-1927," William Lemmon, (1924), http://www.ancestry.com.

372. 1900 U.S. Census, Bergen Co., New Jersey, Englewood, Ward 4, ED 13, p. 11A, dwelling 201, family 222, Mary A. Lemmons.

373. "Georgia Deaths, 1928-1940," database, Marietta, Mary Nelms Lemmon, (1934), https://www.familysearch.org.

374. "United States World War I Registration Cards, 1917-1918," Westmoreland County, Pennsylvania, George Nelms Lemmon, https://www.familysearch.org, FHL 1926976.

375. "Alabama Deaths, 1908-1974," database, Birmingham, George Nelms Lemmon, (1960) https://www.familysearch.org.

376. Isabella McCulloh Lemmon death certificate (1936), "Georgia Deaths, 1928-1940," http://www.ancestry.com.

377. William Presstman Lemmon death certificate (1955), "North Carolina, Death Certificates, 1909-1976," http://www.ancestry.com.

378. 1900 U.S. Census, Bergen Co., New Jersey, Englewood, Ward 4, ED 13, p. 11A, dwelling 201, family 222, Clarita M. Lemmons.

379. Gravestone for Fanny Lemmon (1883-1885), memorial #102372789, http://www.findagrave.com.

380. "U.S. Passport Applications, 1795-1925," Robert S. Lemmon (1910), digital image 994, citing NARA roll 124, 29 Nov. 1910 – 26 Dec. 1910.

381. Gravestone for Robert Stell Lemmon (1885-1964), memorial #136649484, http://www.findagrave.com.

382. "Charles S. McCulloh," obituary, *Richmond Times Dispatch*, 28 December 1940, p. 16, col. 5, http://www.genealogybank.com.

383. "New York Marriages, 1686-1980," index, Manhattan, Charles Sears McCulloh and Kate Monteath Mayo, https://www.familysearch.org.

384. Ibid; McCulloh family papers (no date), privately held by author, 2016.

385. "Marriage Licenses Issued," *Richmond Times Dispatch*, 29 October 1926, p. 22, col. 2, http://www.genealogybank.com.

386. McCulloh family papers (no date), privately held by author, 2016.

387. Ibid; "U.S. Social Security Death Index, 1935-2014," Katharine Scott (1979).

388. "Allan McCulloh" obituary, *New York Times*, 7 May 1932, "Historical Newspapers, Birth, Marriage, & Death Announcements, 1851-2003, http://www.ancestry.com.

389. Gravestone for Robert Lee McCulloh (1860-1922), memorial #126243737, http://www.findagrave.com.

390. "New Jersey Marriages, 1670-1980," database, Englewood, Robt. L. McCulloh and Hetty L. Tilyon, https://www.familysearch.org.

391. "U.S. Passport Applications, 1795-1925," Hetty Tilyon McCulloh, (1894), digital image 1145, citing NARA roll 417, 2 April 1894 – 30 April 1894; "U.S. Newspaper extractions from the Northeast, 1794-1930", *New York Evening Post*, Marriages 1879-1883, p. 91, Robert L. McCulloh and Hetty Louise Tilyou, http://www.ancestry.com.

392. "Ontario, Canada Marriages, 1801-1928," Robert Lee McCulloh, and Eleanor Bell, http://www.ancestry.com.

393. Ibid.

394. Gravestone for Walter McCulloh (1862-1954), memorial # 63824508, http://www.findagrave.com.

395. 1900 U.S. Census, Niagara County, New York, pop. sch., Niagara Falls Ward 1, ED 71, p. 27B, dwelling 474, family 543, Walter. McCulloh, http://www.ancestry.com, citing NARA T623, roll 1129; Gravestone for Caroline Mahala Wright McCulloh (1856-1931), memorial # 63824418, http://www.findagrave.com.

396. 1925 New York State Census, Niagara County, pop. sch., Niagara Falls Ward 2, ED 100, p. 6B, Dorothy McCulloh, http://www.ancestry.com.

397. 1910 U.S. Census, Niagara County, pop. sch., Niagara Falls, Ward 2, AD 04, ED 01, p. 13, Dorothy McCulloh, http://www.ancestry.com; "United States Public Records, 1970-2009," database, Niagara Falls, Dorothy Mcc Smith, https://www.familysearch.org.

398. "Mrs. Dorothy A. McCulloh Smith, 90," obituary, *Buffalo News*, 1 October 1996, http://www.genealogybank.com.

399. "James McCulloh," obituary, *New York Herald*, 6 July 1957, clippings held by author, 2016.

400. "Philadelphia, Pennsylvania Marriage index, 1885-1951," James S. McCulloh and S. May White Gause, (1898), http://www.ancestry.com; "U.S.

Passport Applications, 1795-1925," Mary White McCulloh, (1923), digital image 672, citing NARA roll 2327, 7 July 1923 – 10 July 1923.

401. "Philadelphia, Pennsylvania Marriage index, 1885-1951," Harlan Victor Gause and Sarah May White. (1887); "U.S. Passport Applications, 1795-1925," Harlan Victor Gause, (1921), digital image 672, citing NARA roll 1684, 9 July 1921 – 11 July 1921.

402. Mildred S. White death certificate (1958), "Philadelphia, Pennsylvania, Death Certificates Index, 1906-1963,"

403. Ibid.

404. "New York, New York City Births, 1846-1909," Gordon McCulloh (1899), http://www.familysearch.org, FHL 1953448.

405. Abby Sears Roberts obituary, *New York Times*, 21 May 1934, "Historical Newspapers, Birth, Marriage, & Death Announcements, 1851-2003, http://www.ancestry.com.

406. James DeWolf Hubbard death certificate (1960), "Vermont Death Records, 1909-2008," http://www.ancestry.com.

407. "Pennsylvania, Philadelphia City Births, 1860-1906," R.S. Hubbard, Jr., http://www.familysearch.org, FHL 1289342.

408. "U.S. Passport Applications, 1795-1925," John P. Hubbard, (1923), digital image 592, citing NARA roll 2302, 12 June 1923 – 13 June 1923.

409. James DeWolf Hubbard death certificate (1960), "Vermont Death Records, 1909-2008."

410. Lucy S. Jefferys death certificate (1927), "Pennsylvania, Death Certificates Index, 1906-1963."

411. "Philadelphia, Pennsylvania, Marriage index, 1885-1951," Lucy Sturgis Hubbard and William Hamilton Jefferys.

412. William H. Jefferys death certificate (1945), "Pennsylvania, Death Certificates Index, 1906-1963."

413. 1910 U.S. Census, Philadelphia County, Pennsylvania, pop. sch., Philadelphia, Ward 27, ED 667, p. 4A, dwelling 49, family 50, Nancy Jefferys, http://www.ancestry.com, citing NARA T623, roll 1469.

414. "Florida Death Index, 1877-1998," Lucy Lewis (1971), http://www.ancestry.com.

415. "U.S. Social Security Death Index, 1935-2014," Adelaide J. Garrett (1999).

416. William H. Jefferys, Jr. Death Certificate, "Vermont Death Records, 1909-2008."

417. "Massachusetts Marriages, 1841-1915," database, Lenox, Massachusetts, Sullivan Warren Sturgis and Edith Stuart Barnes, http://www.familysearch.org.

418. "Massachusetts, Town and Vital Records, 1620-1988," Manchester births, 1900, Susan B. Sturgis, http://www.ancestry.com.

419. "U.S. Passport Applications, 1795-1925," Edith Sturgis, (1923), digital image 319, citing NARA roll 2158, 2 January 1923 – 4 January 1923.

420. "U.S. Passport Applications, 1795-1925," Somers Hayes Sturgis, (1922), digital image 29, citing NARA roll 2121, 24 October 1922 – 25 October 1922.

421. "U.S. Social Security Applications and Claims Index, 1936-2007," Warren Sturgis (1997), http://www.ancestry.com.

422. "Massachusetts Death Index, 1901-1980," Milton, Edward Sturgis, http://www.ancestry.com.

423. "Massachusetts, Town Clerk, Vital and Town Records, 1626-2001," Boston, Edward Sturgis and Josephine Putnam, http://www.familysearch.org, FHL 824990.

424. "U.S. Social Security Death Index, 1935-2014," Edward Sturgis (1904).

425. Ibid, George Sturgis (1905).

426. Ibid, Howard O. Sturgis (1906).

427. "Massachusetts, Births Records, 1840-1915," database, Andover, Harriet Lowell Sturgis (1908) http://www.ancestry.com.

428. Ibid, Josephine Lowell Sturgis (1910).

429. "U.S. Social Security Applications and Claims Index, 1936-2007," Charles Russell Sturgis (1913).

430. Gravestone for James McCulloh Sturgis (1872-1959), memorial #144874620, http://www.findagrave.com.

INDEX

A

Alabama
  Anniston 49, 72
  Birmingham 56, 77
Associate Reformed Church
  Baltimore 27
AT&T 60
Austen
  Anna 20, 27, 40, 44, 45, 46, 52, 70
  Caroline (Millemon) 27, 70
  Edward 45
  George 27
  George II 70

B

Baltimore and Ohio Railroad 34
Baltimore United Volunteers 19
Barnes
  Edith Stuart 62, 80
Battle of Bladensburg 19
Battle of Brandywine 4
Battle of Princeton 4
Battle of Trenton 4
Bell
  Eleanor 58, 78
  Emma (Somers) 78
  Thomas 78
Bercegeay
  Adeline 28, 47, 72
  Alphonse 28, 72
  Augustin 55, 76
  Bertha 76
  Bertha M. 55
  Elizabeth (-?-) 72
Billingsport,
  Pa. 4
Booth
  James Curtis 24
Bradley
  Mary Hughes 53, 75
Bringhurst
  Anna 7, 9, 11, 14, 15, 18, 36, 66
  Elizabeth (Shute) 9, 66
  George 12
  John 9, 66
Brown
  Annie (McCulloh) 22, 28, 39, 49, 69, 73
  Susan Theresa 49, 73
  William Isaac 28, 39, 49, 73
  William McCulloh 73
Browne
  Frances 63, 65
Buchanan
  James 32, 33, 34
Buckingham
  Philo 27
Buckingham & McCulloh 27
Buckingham & Sons 27
Burton
  Jessie Olivia 78

C

Canton Company 36
Carroll
  Henry 75
  Mary Stenett 52, 53, 75
  Mary (Winchester) 75
Chesapeake and Ohio Canal 34
Church of the Ascension
  New York City 26
College of New Jersey 24, 28, 68
Colorado
  Denver 54
Columbia College 28, 43, 44, 51, 58

Cross Cut Canal 36
Cummins
  Charles 68
  Margaret (McCulloh) 13, 18, 23, 34, 66, 68

D

Delvaille
  Abby (McCulloh) 47, 56, 72, 77
  Anita 56, 77
  Emile J. 56, 77
  Soline 77
Duer
  Anna Katharine 74
Duffield
  Rev. George 2

E

England
  Charlton 63
Eyre
  Jehu 2, 4

F

First Comptroller of the U.S. 36
Fisher
  Sally 76
Fort Mifflin 2, 3, 4
Fry
  Lucretia 25, 68

G

Gause
  Harlan Victor 79
  Mildred 60
  Sarah May (White) 60, 79
Georgia
  Marietta 56
Green
  Anna 69
  Ashbel (b. 1825) 69
  Isabella (McCulloh) 7, 13
  Isabella (McCulloh) (b. 1793) 36, 67, 69
  Isabella W. (b. 1834) 69
  Jacob 68
  James Sprout 37, 69
  James Sprout, Jr. 69
  Mary (McCulloh) 13, 18, 66, 68
  Rev. Ashbel 68, 69
  Robert Stockton 69
Greene
  Belle 50, 76
  Henry Copley 55, 76
  Isabella (McCulloh) (b. 1825) 21, 22, 24, 25, 26, 39, 49, 54, 69, 71
  John Singleton Copley, Jr. 54, 55, 76
  John Singleton Copley, Rev. 26, 39, 71, 76
  Margaret 72
  Mary Emery 72
  Mary (Mayer) 54, 55, 64, 71, 76
  Mary (McCulloh) 50

H

Harvard University 24, 55, 62
Howland and Aspinwall 27
Hubbard
  Adelaide (McCulloh) 22, 25, 26, 49, 69, 73
  Anne 49, 73
  Edith 49, 73
  Elizabeth (Perry) 79
  James DeWolf 79
  Jane 49, 73
  John P. (b. 1853) 26
  John P. (b. 1860) 26, 73
  John P. (b. 1903) 79
  John P., Rev. 26, 49, 73
  Lucy Sturgis 61, 73, 79
  Margaret 26, 73
  Mary 49, 73
  Rev. John P. 25, 49

Russell Sturgis 61, 73, 79
Russell Sturgis, Jr. 79
William 26

I

Immanuel Episcopal Church 51, 52
  Cemetery 44, 46, 69, 70, 75
Iowa
  Muscatine 68
Irving
  Abby (McCulloch) 46, 51, 52, 70, 74
  Anna 74
  Anna (Duer) 74
  Elizabeth Kip 51, 74
  John Duer 74
  Peter 74
  Pierre Frederick 74
  Pierre Paris 51, 74
  Roland Duer 51, 52, 74

J

Jefferson College 24
Jefferys
  Adelaide 61
  Adelaide McCulloh 79
  Lucy 61, 79
  Lucy (Hubbard) 73, 79
  Nancy 79
  William Hamilton 61, 79
  William H., Jr. 79

K

Kennedy
  John Pendleton 19
Knox
  William 18
Knox, Usher and McCulloh 6

L

Labordaire
  Galatee 69

Leavenworth
  Eunice 75
  Franklin 75
  Jane 53, 75
Lemmon
  Caroline (McCulloh) 56, 72, 77
  Clarita M. 77
  George Nelms 56, 77
  Isabel McCulloh 77
  Mary Nelms 77
  Robert Stell 77
  Susan (-?-) 77
  William (b. 1836) 56, 77
  William P. 77
  William Presstman (b. 1878) 56, 77
Lewis
  George T. 76
  Mary Fisher 76
  Sally (Fisher) 76
Louisiana
  Ascension Parish 28, 55, 72
  Donaldsonville 76
  New Orleans 47, 66, 77
Louisiana State University 44

M

Maryland
  Glencoe 45, 75
Massachusetts
  Brookline 26, 40, 71, 74, 76
  Groton 62
  Manchester 40, 74
  Milton 62
  Newton 54, 72
  Northampton 26
  Worthington 73
Matthews
  Fanny 29
  George 29
  John 29
  Martha 29
  Mary 29

Sarah 29
William 29
Mayer
    Charles F. 70
    Christina 76
    Ethel M. 76
    George 76
    Henry C. (b. 1883) 76
    Henry Christian (b. 1821) 24, 70
    Henry Christian (b. 1844) 24, 54, 71, 76
    Mary Abby 50, 54, 55, 64, 71, 76
    Mary (Lewis) 76
    Mary (McCulloh) 21, 22, 24, 39, 40, 49, 50, 54, 69, 70
    Nina (Stevens) 54, 76
    Susan Theresa 24, 71
Mayo
    Kate Monteath 56, 78
    Marie Louise (Ritter) 78
    Sylvanus 78
McBlair
    Elizabeth 65
McCulloch
    Abby Louise 46, 51, 52, 70, 74
    Anna (Austen) (b. 1823) 20, 27, 40, 44, 45, 46, 52, 70
    Anna (b. 1848) 46, 70
    Anna (b. 1903) 75
    Caroline Austen 46, 70
    Duncan (b. 1853) 46, 52, 53, 70, 75
    Duncan (b. 1898) 75
    Edward Austen 70
    Elizabeth Duncan 75
    Elizabeth (Irving) 51, 74
    George (b. 1845) 51, 70, 74
    George Sears 51, 52
    James W. (b. 1857) 53, 70, 75
    Jane (Leavenworth) 53, 75
    John Austen 54, 70, 75
    John Sears (b. 1816) 21, 23, 24, 27, 36, 39, 41, 44, 46, 52, 68, 69
    Margaret Callender 75
    Mary (Bradley) 53, 75
    Mary (Carroll) 52, 53, 75
    Mary (Tyson) 54, 75
    Mary Winchester Carroll 75
    Paul Leavenworth 75
    Robet Austen 74
    Warren Sturgis 75
McCulloch v. Maryland 32, 33
McCulloh
    Abby Sears (b. 1865) 47, 56, 72, 77
    Abby Sears (b. 1870) 49, 61, 64, 73, 79
    Abigail (Sears) 19, 21, 24, 25, 37, 39, 41, 68
    Adelaide Sears 22, 25, 26, 49, 69, 73
    Adeline (Bercegeay) 28, 47
    Allan 58, 64, 72, 78
    Andrew 7, 12, 13, 14, 18, 66
    Anna (Bringhurst) 7, 9, 11, 14, 15, 18, 36, 66
    Anna (Todd) 1, 13, 66
    Anne (b. 1779) 66
    Anne (b. 1799) 13, 67
    Anne (c. 1765) 65, 67
    Anne Eliza 68
    Annie Lucretia 22, 28, 39, 49, 69, 73
    Archy 72
    Bertha (Bercegeay) 55, 56, 76
    Caroline (b. 1825) 56
    Caroline (b. 1852) 56, 72, 77
    Caroline (Wright) 58, 59, 78
    Charles Sears 27, 56, 57, 58, 72, 78
    Chlorine 69
    Dorothy 78
    Dr. Samuel (b. 1772) 7, 13, 14, 15, 21, 29, 34, 35, 36, 63, 66, 68
    Eleanor 63, 64, 66, 68
    Eleanor (b. 1798) 67
    Eleanor (Bell) 78
    Elizabeth Ann (b. 1822) 21, 34, 69
    Elizabeth (b. 1776) 13, 66

Elizabeth (McBlair) 65
Frances (b. 1770-72) 63, 66
Frances (Browne) 63, 65
Frances (Roupell) 63, 65
Francis (b. 1770) 66
Galatee (Labordaire) 69
George 69
George (b. 1791) 13, 67
Gordon 60, 79
Hannah (Williams) 66
Hetty Louise (Tilyon) 78
Isaac 13, 22, 67
Isabella (b. 1793) 7, 13, 36, 67, 69
Isabella (b. 1825) 21, 22, 24, 25, 26, 39, 49, 54, 69, 71
Isabella (Walker) 27, 47, 49, 58, 61, 72
Isabella (Williamson) (b. 1803) 1, 68
Isabella Williamson (b. 1825) 26, 39, 49
Isabelle 69
James (b. 1857) 72
James (c. 1754) 1, 6, 18, 65, 67
James Sears 59, 60, 61, 73, 78
James W. (b. 1789) 1, 6, 9, 11, 12, 13, 15, 18, 19, 20, 22, 23, 24, 26, 28, 29, 34, 35, 36, 37, 39, 40, 41, 63, 66, 68
    career 6, 15, 31
    characteristics 27
    First Comptroller 24, 36, 37
    foreclosure 21, 33
    home in Baltimore 21
    home in Philadelphia 11
    Maryland Speaker of the House 34
    McCulloch vs Maryland 32, 33
    speculating 32
    teenager 16, 17
James W. (b. 1827) 22, 27, 28, 47, 48, 49, 61, 69, 72
James William Benoi Todd. *See* Mc-
Culloh, James W. (b. 1789)
Jessie Olivia (Burton) 78
John (b. 1721) 65
John (b. 1747) 1, 5, 6, 7, 9, 13, 14, 15, 18, 41, 63, 65, 66
    death 12
    house 10, 11
    pension 4
    Revolutionary War 2-4
    Western lands 6, 35
    will 13
John (b. 1784) 13, 18
John Sears (b. 1816). *See* McCulloch
Joseph 6, 65
Josephine 69
Kate (Mayo) 56, 78
Katharine Mayo 78
Margaret (b. 1787) 13, 18, 23, 34, 66, 68
Margaret (b. 1834) 22, 24, 39, 40, 69, 74
Margaret (d. 1784) 66
Margaretta Grace 28, 70
Margie 47, 72
Mary (b. 1782) 12, 13, 18, 66, 68
Mary Eaton 58, 72
Mary Louisa (b. 1821) 21, 22, 24, 39, 40, 49, 50, 54, 64, 69, 70
Mary (Vowell) 28, 70
Mildred Gause 60, 79
Peggy (- ? -) 67
Richard (b. 1883) 77
Richard McCall 47, 55, 56, 72, 76
Richard Sears (b. 1818) 21, 23, 24, 28, 39, 43, 44, 69, 70
Robert (b. 1742) 63, 65
Robert (b. 1795) 13
Robert (b. 1860) 58, 72, 78
Robert Pierce 67
Samuel 65, 68
Sarah (b. 1792) 13, 35, 67
Sarah (c. 1761) 65, 67

Sarah (White) 60, 79
Walter 58, 59, 72, 78
William (b. 1748) 6
William (b. 1800) 35, 67, 69
William (b. 1827) 72
William (c. 1748) 65, 66
William James (b. 1827) 22, 24, 28, 29, 46, 47, 69
William J. (b. 1892) 77
McDowell
  Elizabeth 66
McMahon
  John V. L. 27
Millemon
  Caroline 27, 70
Morris
  William Lewis 27

N

New Jersey
  Englewood 47, 61, 77
  Orange 28, 39, 53, 75
  Princeton 69
New Jersey Midland Railroad 28
New York
  New Brighton 51
  New York City 27, 28, 37, 39, 48, 49, 56, 58, 72
  Niagara Falls 58, 78
  Riverdale 27
  Rye 61
  Southfield 27
  Yonkers 78
New York City. *See* New York
New York Telephone Company 59, 60

O

Oldfields School 44, 51, 52, 53, 54
Old Pine Church. *See* Third Presbyterian Church

P

Panic of 1819 32
Pannell
  Ann Pierce 67
  Edward 6, 67
  Edward (b. 1794) 67
  Elizabeth 67
  George Washington 67
  Hugh 67
  James 67
  Jane 67
  Sarah 67
  Sarah (McCulloh) 67
  William 67
Pennsylvania
  Pittsburgh 7
  Tracts of land in Western 6, 14, 35, 36, 41
  Western 7, 35
Perry
  Elizabeth 79
Pierce
  Anna (Williamson) 68
  Humphrey 68
  Levi 68
  Mary Elizabeth (Williamson) 68
Princeton Theological Seminary 68
Princeton University. *See* College of New Jersey
Putnam
  Josephine 62, 80

R

Revolutionary War 2, 3, 4, 6
Rhode Island
  Newport 68
  Westerly 26, 73
Ritter
  Marie Louise 78
Roberts
  Abby (McCulloh) 49, 61, 64, 73, 79

Arthur Lloyd 61, 79
Rockland 29, 63
Roupell
　Frances 63, 65
　Frances (McCulloh) 63
　George 63
　George Boone 63

S

Scotland
　Kirkcudbright 66
Sears
　Abigail 19, 21, 24, 25, 37, 39, 41, 68
　George 19, 68
　Lucretia (Fry) 25, 68
Second Bank of the United States 31, 32, 33, 34
Shoemaker
　Mary (Tyson) 54, 75
Shute
　Elizabeth 9, 66
Slaves 21, 29
　Emery 29
　Harriett 29
　Mary Ann 29
Sleepy Hollow Cemetery 74
Smith
　David 29
　Dick 29
　James 29
　Jane 29
　Jim 29
　Maria 29
　Suck 29
Somers
　Emma 78
Steel
　Caroline Lydia 72
Stevens
　Nina Coppee 54, 76
Stokes
　Anson Phelps 53

Sturgis
　Charles Russell 80
　Edith (b. 1903) 62, 80
　Edith (Barnes) 62, 80
　Edward (b. 1868) 62, 74, 80
　Edward J. (b. 1904) 80
　George Putnam 80
　Harriet Lowell 80
　Howard O. 80
　James McCulloh 40, 62, 74, 80
　Josephine Lowell 80
　Josephine (Putnam) 62, 80
　Lucy Codman 40, 74
　Margaret (McCulloh) 22, 24, 39, 40, 69, 74
　Russell, Jr. 40, 74
　Somers Hayes 62, 80
　Sullivan Warren 62, 74, 80
　Susan B. 80
　Warren 62, 80
Sunny Waters 40

T

Third Presbyterian Church 1, 2
　cemetery 6, 13, 66
Tilyon
　Emma (-?-) 78
　Hetty Louise 78
　Vincent 78
Todd
　Andrew 66
　Anna 1, 13, 66
　Elizabeth (McDowell) 66
Trinity Church
　Baltimore 25
Tyson
　Elizabeth W. 76
　James W. 76
　Mary Dawson 54, 75

U

University of Louisiana 55

University of Maryland 23, 36
Upham
  Henry 40, 49, 71
  Mary (McCulloh) 21, 22, 24, 39, 49,
    50, 54, 64, 70

V

Virginia Military Institute 55
Vowell
  John D. 28
  Mary Stewart 28, 70

W

Walker
  Caroline (Steel) 72
  Isabella Steel 27, 47, 49, 61, 72
  William 72
War of 1812 19
Wave Hill 27
West Virginia
  Potomac 26
White
  Sarah May 79
Williams
  George 18, 32, 33, 34
  Hannah 66
Williamson
  Anna 68
  Anne (McCulloh) 67
  David 67
  Isabella 68
  Isabella (b. 1803) 1
  Mary Elizabeth 68
Winchester
  Mary 75
Wright
  Caroline 58, 59, 78
  Christina (-?-) 78
  George 78

www.ingramcontent.com/pod-product-compliance
Lightning Source LLC
Chambersburg PA
CBHW072052290426
44110CB00014B/1650